£6-50

WHERE IS
HE NOW?
The Extraordinary Worlds of Edward James

(Avery Danziger)

WHERE IS HE NOW?

The Extraordinary Worlds of Edward James

PHILIP PURSER

QUARTET BOOKS
LONDON   MELBOURNE   NEW YORK

First published by Quartet Books Limited 1978
A member of the Namara Group
27 Goodge Street, London W1P 1FD
Copyright © 1978 by Philip Purser
ISBN 0 7043 2167 X
Design by Mike Jarvis

Printed in Great Britain by litho at
The Anchor Press Ltd and bound by
Wm Brendon & Son Ltd, both of
Tiptree, Essex

ACKNOWLEDGEMENTS

The lines from John Betjeman's *Summoned by Bells* are reproduced by permission of
the author and Messrs John Murray; the extract from *The Gardener Who Saw God* by
permission of Messrs Duckworth; that from 'Shut Gates' in *The Bones of My Hand*
by permission of the author. Other quotations from Edward James's verse
are taken from privately printed or circulated editions, with his permission.
For access to these editions, and other assistance, I am grateful to Mr M. Heymann,
F.R.I.C.S., Agent to the West Dean Estate, and to Mrs F. E. Lanchester,
Librarian of West Dean College. Mr Patrick Boyle and A.T.V. Network Ltd
kindly made available recordings or transcripts from their television documentary
about Edward James. In California I was much helped by Mr and Mrs Gustave Field
and Mr Jack Larson. My thanks, finally, to the subject of this book, for his time,
patience and several polychromatic missives.

INTRODUCTION

In the summer of 1945 two men were travelling in Mexico with packs and sleeping bags piled in the back of the car. It was at that pause in history when the war in Europe was over but a long slog, everyone thought, still lay ahead against Japan. The two had driven down through New Mexico as unconscious as the rest of the world of the awesome weapon being assembled in the desert there. The news of Hiroshima, and then of Nagasaki, was to break in a few days' time. For the moment, as they followed a rough road into the eastern Sierra Madre, the War, and indeed the whole civilization at stake in the War, seemed absurdly remote. The sky was an intense blue; on each side of the road was jungle; ahead, the peaks beckoned. They crossed the Rio Santa Maria by primitive ferry and on the bank of one of its tributaries stopped for a swim.

One of the men was a sergeant in the American army, a good-looking, cheerful Texan with Indian blood. For him the impact of Mexico was – or should have been – total, because he was on leave after two years in the Aleutians, foggy sub-Arctic islands whose name alone was enough to signify an unenviable posting in the songs and radio shows of the day, and he had hardly seen the sun in that time, let alone sweltered in its heat. His companion was short and smooth-skinned, looking much younger than his age, which was nearly thirty-eight. He was the driving force of the expedition; it was his car, his money, his pursuit of the romantic and the exotic which determined their wanderings – just now, into the mountains in search of wild orchids said to run riot in the valley below a curious hook-shaped peak called Huestmolotepl.

He was, of course, Edward James, and in a sense this journey was a model of his whole life until then, full of enthusiasms, yearnings and passionate attachments which were never quite fulfilled. Even his relationship with the Texan, Roland McKenzie, was under a certain strain. Their sensibilities were too different. Just as distant clouds had parted to give a first glimpse of Huestmolotepl like a cocked thumb on the skyline, the soldier had destroyed the moment for James by blowing cigarette smoke, for God's sake, across his face.

By the river now, though, it was idyllic enough. Edward was sunning himself after his swim. McKenzie came out of the water, naked, grinning. On the bank was a big patch of bright blue and yellow flowers. He jumped into the middle of it, and the flowers exploded into the air. They were giant butterflies. They wheeled and swirled and as they began to settle again did an extraordinary thing: attracted perhaps by the smell of wet flesh they settled on the Texan until he was clothed in butterflies, like a cheerful, clowning, Mayan God. The vision remains imprinted on the mind of Edward James as the one perfect realization – or surrealization – of something which he has sought all his life.

If you are born extremely rich but uninterested in power or making more money,

what is there to drive you on? If nevertheless you write or draw or compose, nothing much less than genius will get you taken seriously – the rich man's well-advertised difficulty in gaining the Kingdom of Heaven is child's play by the side of his trying to make the Republic of Letters. If you display an undeniable flair for being right about pictures and the pictures you spotted were surrealist, how tempting to take refuge in the surrealist belief that art is the product of accident, and the artist is merely the one who can recognize beauty and magic when they are offered.

James has flitted in and out of the fringes of history this half century while (so far) remaining curiously unknown, considering that he spurred on such painters as Dali, Magritte and Tchelitchew, inspired a ballet by Brecht and Weill, was married to (and luridly divorced from) one of the most beautiful women in Europe, lived for years in Hollywood, owns a unique art collection, has endowed a college and is just possibly the Queen of England's bastard great-uncle. He crops up in all sorts of memoirs, from Edith Sitwell's to Tom Driberg's, but isn't in *Who's Who*. The spotlight has picked him out briefly, then he has vanished again into mysterious exile. John Betjeman, who owes the first publication of his verse to James, asked in his autobiographical *Summoned by Bells*, 'But where's he now? What does he do?'

Where he is, mostly, is in Mexico again. What he is doing there is trying to re-create, literally and astonishingly in concrete terms, that vision of butterflies.

The Mountain beckons:
Huestmolotepl (*Plutarco Gastelum*)

ONE

The Court Circular for November 19, 1906, reported that the King had left the Palace that afternoon for West Dean Park, Chichester, to honour Mr and Mrs W. James with a visit. Edward Frank Willis James was born on August 16, 1907, thus lending arithmetical support to the widely-held belief that he is the illegitimate son of Edward VII. Certainly that gamey old monarch was very fond of Mrs James, and, at a time when it was unusual for a king to lodge with a commoner, stayed frequently at West Dean Park. It is also a fact that he stood as the boy's godfather, and presented him with a gold goblet bearing his name. But Edward James can produce some reasonable quibbles with the story and a plausible alternative to it. He says that the King never came alone; if he wasn't accompanied by Queen Alexandra he brought Mrs Keppel, his accepted mistress; under either circumstance any philandering would have been out of the question. Nor was Willie James the kind of man to accept the rôle of *mari complaisant*. Finally, and conclusively to Edward's satisfaction, his mother left him a bundle of letters from the King indicating a very different relationship. He was not her lover but her father! Her mother had been brought up on a Scottish estate bordering the royal estate at Balmoral. What likelier happening than a little hanky-panky in the heather with a younger and notoriously sprightly Prince of Wales some time around 1870? In which case Edward James is his father's son with a royal intrusion only into the maternal line.

Assuming this version, he is descended from a family either Lancastrian or Irish in origin (there is some disagreement) which had emigrated to America by the end of the 18th century. The James riches came at first from timber – Edward's great-grandfather bought up vast tracts of woodland in New York State, and Edward says his own passion for planting trees must come from some instinct to redress his ancestor's wholesale felling. This man's son, Daniel James, is the key figure in subsequent genealogy. He married first into the Phelps Dodge family, thereby adding rich mining interests to the timber, and left the children of his marriage in America to continue the American branch of the family. He then re-married and came to England in 1847 to start up what became the English branch. He settled at Woolton, near Liverpool, handy for the transatlantic steamers by which he maintained control of his business, and had three sons. Frank grew up to be an explorer and big game hunter, duly killed by an elephant. Arthur was a well-known racehorse owner. William Dodge James, always known as Willie, was content – after he had acquired West Dean Park and its 10,000 acres – to be described as a landowner.

Photographs dating from the turn of the century show a handsome, rather ordinary face with heavy moustache and hair brushed back from a lofty brow. He was also something of a traveller, with an ocean-going yacht, *Lancashire Witch*, and a sportsman. His prowess as a shot, not to mention the acres of shooting now at his

King Edward VII, posed in front of West Dean's
unmistakable Sussex flint facade.
Portrait by F. W. Swaine.
(*Robin Constable*)

Mrs Willie, with Xandra and Sylvia (the smaller
girl) in the beautiful Robert Brough group
hanging in the library at West Dean. (*Robin
Constable*)

disposal, provided the enduring basis of his friendship with Edward VII. Mrs Willie
James, *née* Evelyn Forbes, was a pretty, doll-like woman who to tease the King once
pretended in fact to be a doll, lying motionless, with bright rouged cheeks, in tissue
paper in a giant cardboard box. There were four daughters spread over a dozen
years, which everyone assumed would be the extent of the family. A fine outdoor
group by Robert Brough (who might have been more famous if he hadn't died
young) hanging in the library at West Dean depicts the mother, elegant in white,
with two of the little girls, Xandra and Sylvia. Then to everyone's surprise, and the
chagrin of some, Edward arrived.

He was born into a world of luxury, leisure and the ever-attendance of servants
which even the costume serials on television have never fully evoked. Mrs Willie

The companion portrait of William Dodge
James. Both pictures must have been painted not
long before Brough's untimely death in 1905 at
the age of thirty-three. (*Robin Constable*)

James had a personal footman whose only duty was to hand her anything she wanted
and pick up anything she dropped. The children were brought up by nannies and
governesses. When their mother once sent for a child to accompany her to church
and was asked which one, she is supposed to have snapped, 'How should I know?
Whichever one goes with my blue gown.' She was dressed by Worth, and Edward
says that in an age of not particularly becoming fashions she always managed to
look beautiful. He remembers oyster silks, high chokers of pearls, little bunches of
Parma violets pinned to furs, and the letters she was constantly writing in blue ink
on blue paper to her friends and relatives and gossips.

The seasons of the year were marked by stately progresses from West Dean to
the town house in Bryanston Square and thence to Greywalls, on the Firth of Forth

Page of the West Dean visitors' book from 1899 has a photograph pasted over the guest list at a summer house-party – probably Goodwood week. In the light-coloured billycock hat is Edward VII again; by his side, Mrs Willie. (*Robin Constable*)

From an earlier year, 1892, the page relating to a
pheasant-shooting weekend has cartoon
decorations thought to be by Mrs Willie herself.
(*Robin Constable*)

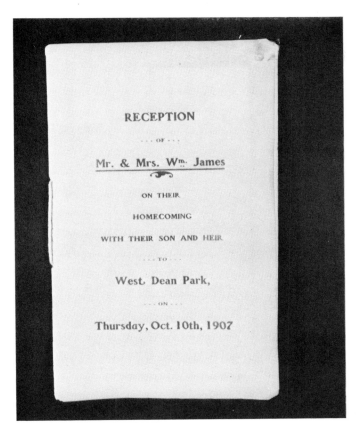

RECEPTION

··· OF ···

Mr. & Mrs. Wᵐ· James

ON THEIR

HOMECOMING

WITH THEIR SON AND HEIR

··· TO ···

West Dean Park,

··· ON ···

Thursday, Oct. 10th, 1907

Cover of the eight-page
programme to the festivities
marking the homecoming of
the two-month-old Master
Edward. He received a loyal
address from locals, nine
pieces of gold plate and a
firework display. (*Robin
Constable*)

near Edinburgh, where the late summer would be spent and where Edward, as it happened, was born. His homecoming to West Dean at age of two months was the occasion for a grand ceremony with fireworks and music. It was also at Greywalls that Edward claims to have registered his first interest in art, at the age of three. They'd been visiting Lord and Lady Wemyss at Gosford and everyone had admired a Botticelli of the infant Jesus which was the pride of the Wemyss collection. Next day Edward was found by his nurse lying in a curious position. 'Master Edward, what are you doing?' 'I'm being a bottled cherry.' From the same summer he dates, perhaps more fancifully, the exercise of his imagination which was later to make him a surrealist. Thought to be a delicate child, he was sent to bed early. In the mornings he had to stay there until a nursemaid came to free him from his brass-railed cot. Lying awake, listening frustratedly to the surf and the seabirds, he turned his bed into a flying castle, a palace under the sea, a tower rising up through the trees.

These very early years have – rather touchingly, since he can't have remembered very much from them – become the golden years in Edward's estimation. For when he was only five his father died after being taken ill on a trip to South Africa, and the prison house shades closed in. The family was in London at the time. Edward

West Dean as it
looked in 1890.

was packed off to stay with bleak old kinsman, Lord Wolverton. He remembers
sobbing and sobbing when told he would never see his father again. Worse, from
his grief his mother suddenly realized that she occupied no comparable position in
his affections; he was much fonder of his nurse; after all, she fed and washed and
looked after him. The nurse was dismissed. It was, says Edward, like being doubly
bereaved.

TWO

The estate that Edward inherited from his father turned out to consist, rather literally,
of the West Dean estate. Though Willie Dodge James had been an extremely
wealthy man, the wealth was tied up either in his property in Britain or in stocks in

America – to the timber and mining interests old Daniel had added a massive investment in the railways as they opened up the continent, and the family now owned something like a seventh of the entire American railroad system. What wasn't to hand was ready cash, and the death duties lately introduced by Lloyd George were unfortunately required – at that time – to be paid in cash. So much railway stock had to be sold at once that its value dipped. After generous provision for the widow (who remarried quite shortly) and the four daughters, Edward was left with only a few hundred a year and those sprawling, costly acres. His trustees

A student craftsman
at work. (*The Times*)

The scope of the Edward James
collection – from the Renaissance
to the twentieth-century. (*Daily
Telegraph Colour Library*)

let the house and grounds and to raise money for his education sold off large parcels
of the remaining land. He was a rich child, yes, but no longer the heir to buoyant,
self-renewing riches that he might once have seemed. He claims today that all his life
he has lived on capital.

He did not take possession of West Dean until he was a young man, and then
only lived there for a total of four or five years; however it remains the seat by
which he is identified in Burke's *Landed Gentry* and the object of a great deal of his
concern. Willie James acquired the estate in 1890 from a Mr Bower who had bought

it from the Peachey family, the Earls of Selsey. Even reduced, these days, to six
thousand five hundred acres, it reaches over a sizeable chunk of Sussex downland
north of Chichester. To the east it adjoins the Duke of Richmond's Goodwood
estate; the crowds that throng the Trundle, the famous hill overlooking the finishing
post on Goodwood race course, are only half a mile from West Dean House. About
a third of the land is farmed directly, another third let to tenant farmers, the rest woodland. Getting on for two hundred acres are leased to the Nature Conservancy.
One of the English vineyards which have been planted in recent years occupies
another corner. There is an open-air museum of rural life for which Edward donated
the land, and he retains some five hundred acres for his own use, including an
arboretum.

The house dates originally from Elizabethan times but was greatly extended,
and 'Gothicized' by James Wyatt about 1790, with a flinty grey façade and mock
battlements. John Piper once suggested to Edward, who considered the idea for a
while, that he should strip away the Gothic features to leave what Piper said would
be a perfect Georgian house. A proposal which appealed more durably arose when
West Dean Church, which in the feudal fashion nestles under the walls of the big
house, was almost destroyed by fire in 1934. Why not rebuild it in a style to match
the house? Edward went to the Soane Museum and found among the designs of
Sir John Soane one for a City church, anticipating the Gothic Revival, which in fact
was never built. John Betjeman knew an architect who was willing to adapt the
plans to what remained of the old church. Edward offered to bear the extra cost.
Alas, the churchwardens turned down the scheme. It was shortly after Edward had
been involved with his ballet season and, said the local virago, 'We don't want any
of Mr James's Russian ballet nonsense down here in Sussex.'

It was the same, he says, when only a few years ago now he wanted to build a
model village close by the church. West Dean, he argued, had always lacked a proper
focus as a village – it straggled here and there. Also, more housing was needed for
estate employees. He would build dwellings in traditional Sussex brick-and-flint style
grouped round a traditional village green. On this occasion local planning authorities
turned down the scheme.

The house had been let latterly to an elderly brother-in-law of Edward's. His
eldest sister Millicent had married one of the Mowbray Howards, the Duke of
Norfolk's family; they had West Dean Park at a peppercorn rent. When Edward
finally moved in he found it too big and too costly to run. If his wife had taken to
the place, perhaps . . . but she preferred town life, and the only memento of her
brief occupancy is a spiral staircase still carpeted with a pattern of bare feet. Edward,
typically, had it woven from a wet footprint she left as she stepped out of the bath.

There were two alternative residences on the estate: Binderton House, a pretty
little Queen Anne manor house which was let during the Second World War years
to Anthony Eden and has lately been sold; and Monkton House, built in a remote
outpost of the property by Willie James as a shooting lodge and occasional annexe
for children and nannies when there was a big house party at West Dean itself.
Edward chose Monkton, with consequences that will be surveyed presently. The

problem of what to do with the big house remained. The Duke of Westminster and Lord Camrose, the newspaper peer, were both prospective purchasers for a while. Edward hatched some rather wild ideas, including one to make it a distant department of Pekin University. But in the end it was let again. During the war it housed the offices of Butterworths, the legal publishers. For thirteen years it was a girls' school, Wispers. Finally Edward made it over to the Edward James Foundation, which he had set up in 1964, and in 1970 it opened as West Dean College, an independent adult college for the crafts.

Up to one hundred students are resident at a time, taking courses in everything from cane seating to calligraphy and illumination, from pottery to blacksmithing and wrought iron work. Most of these last only ten days, five days, even a weekend, and it can't be denied that there is a slight Women's Institutish air to the enterprise. It isn't exactly what Edward dreamed of when he proposed the college: he had a romantic desire to re-establish such crafts as stone carving and decorative plasterwork as full-time occupations, rather overlooking the inconvenient fact that there is only a limited call for these skills. But there are professional courses, lasting a year, in antique furniture and clock restoration. The Victoria and Albert Museum, Edward

Edward painted by O. Greenwood at about the age of twenty. It hangs in the day nursery at West Dean. Edward disowns the hands, which look very large and meat-like. (*Robin Constable*)

says proudly, sends pieces to be repaired by the students, though he can't resist adding that so do antique-dealers.

The Edward James Foundation, which administers the farms as tenancies and a vast art collection as well as the college, and employs a total of one hundred people, represents an endowment of something in the order of £10 million by Edward. Nothing makes him more indignant (and many things make him indignant) than the assumption it was all a tax fiddle. He claims that he had plentiful opportunities over the years to sell up and shift the capital abroad. He was resident in America, at one time in the process of becoming an American citizen; and the money, after all, had come from America in the first place.

If weekend schools of basket-weaving seem a rather slender end-product from so much investment, the demand for places at the college indicates it is filling a need. It is also attracting an increasing number of closed courses and conferences. Noel Simon, a local writer and a Trustee of the Foundation, has no doubt that one day the College will be recognized as one of the most imaginative creations of its kind. For the student arriving at West Dean, or the delegate attending one of the conferences, there is always the added attraction, if he is so interested, of a sensation of life in a great house from *Upstairs, Downstairs* days. The big old bedrooms have been skilfully divided to preserve their character as much as possible. The great Oak Hall, with carvings by a legendary craftsman and his son, the Englishes, is now the students' common room. On the walls hang the tapestries that Willie James collected, and maps and paintings of his yacht and vague, dark old portraits. Half close your eyes and it is not too difficult to visualize Mrs Willie in her favourite nook, footman to hand, scribbling those letters in blue ink on blue paper, or to imagine a small, rather beautiful boy, wandering through the subterranean corridors, a lone child in a grown-up world.

THREE

Schooldays, which the English upper classes tend to sentimentalize, Edward found refreshingly horrible. His mother had picked his prep school on snobbish rather than practical grounds, e.g. hygiene. Indeed she preferred to believe that bodily functions did not exist. The school had eight lavatories for eighty boys and allowed only ten minutes between breakfast and the first lesson. Aided by the school diet Edward became chronically constipated. His mother over-reacted during the holidays and called in a surgeon who, like the Harley Street smoothies in *The Doctor's Dilemma*, had lately developed his private speciality. At the age of twelve Edward lost a length of his intestine in the first of the many operations to which his seventy-year-old abdomen bears witness.

Eton he liked little better; the lessons bored him and he learned more from friends, in particular a boy called John Lawrence (now Sir John, the linguist and Russian scholar) who had an enthusiasm for Renaissance art and had read all Dostoyevsky. Harold Acton was also in Edward's house but Edward found his brand of aestheticism too cloying. He was still a country landowner's son who enjoyed hunting and was a good shot, though already beginning to dislike the idea of taking life. At the age of fifteen he wrote a poem, *Lines Written on the Butt of My Gun*, lamenting the need to kill in order to live. His mother found it, for she allowed no privacy – not even a lock on his door – and when he retrieved it much later she had noted in the margin, 'Very morbid. Must show to Florrie Bridges,' Florrie Bridges being a neighbour and confidante and the wife of a 'no-nonsense' general.

Mrs Willie's new husband seems to have made no impression on Edward, and he rarely even mentions his step-father. To his mother he obviously did remain close, but without much love being lost on either side. The picture he paints of her from his childhood is hardly flattering. The doll-like prettiness was becoming exaggerated by a thyroid deficiency which gave her rather protuberant eyes. She lived in grand style but harboured premonitions of revolution, and would descend on cottagers with calves-foot jelly and cast-off clothes in the vague hope of insuring her own immunity. Edward concedes that she was a brilliant and tireless organizer if a good cause attracted her attention. During the First World War she first raised the money for, and ran, two facial-injury hospitals for the troops, then a scheme to provide lodgings for officers' widows, whose pensions – she had discovered – often took months to come through. She was also, all her life, a fine needlewoman who embroidered her own curtains.

Her reluctance to acknowledge the facts of digestion extended to other facts of life. Edward has said his sisters knew so little about sex they all had alarming wedding nights. A similar lack of imagination on her part helped to bring about the incident which gave him a certain boyhood notoriety – Tom Driberg does not fail to attach it to the reference to Edward in his memoirs, themselves notorious, published under the title *Ruling Passions*. A Liberal politician called Lord Harcourt who was a friend of Mrs Willie's apparently had a weakness for young boys. Edward kept his distance, but after he and his mother had stayed at his country house one weekend, and were about to leave on the Monday morning, she insisted that he go up and thank their host in his bedroom. Edward descended again hurriedly and on the verge of tears. In the motor car going home she scolded him for his lack of politeness until finally he blurted out the truth.

That evening, says Edward, she donned a dressing gown, hid her hair in a silk cap and arranged herself in a suitably grave pose in order to deliver a solemn warning against the dangers of evil men, whom she listed as Nero, Heliogobalus, Benvenuto Cellini – who had actually proclaimed the offence in writing! – Oscar Wilde and now Lord Harcourt. She also complained so loudly about him to her friends that the luckless man was disgraced, and eventually met his death in circumstances calling for an inquest. The jury recorded a verdict of misadventure.

In West Dean days Mrs Willie James had patronized the American cousins who came visiting. Poor Harriet James who had called to Edward VII, as he went out with a gun, 'Good hunting, Your Majesty!' was endlessly teased, which may have contributed to the anti-British sentiments of her husband, the incredibly wealthy Arthur Curtis James, with dire consequences for Edward. In 1923, however, Mrs James and her unmarried daughters went off to America and found the home comforts of the cousins – in New York City and Newport, Rhode Island, and Florida – so agreeable that they stayed for month after month, and were only persuaded to take their leave, says Edward, by the tactful gift of sets of handmade, monogrammed luggage all round.

Edward had remained at Eton, but for the last year or two of his schooling was able to escape to the more agreeable surroundings of an expensive private establishment in Switzerland. His mother had misgivings at first but was characteristically won over when she discovered his room-mate was a German princeling. Oxford loomed pleasurably ahead.

FOUR

Charting his upward progress through undergraduate society in *Summoned by Bells*, John Betjeman confesses:

> Week after sunny week
> I climbed, still keeping in, I thought, with God,
> Until I reached what seemed to me the peak –
> The leisured set in Canterbury Quad.

Canterbury Quad is, or was, the richest precinct of the richest Oxford college, Christ Church. Originally it was a college in its own right, for Benedictine scholars from Canterbury. The present buildings date from the same period as West Dean House, indeed were built by the same architect, Wyatt, which should have helped Edward James feel at home when he arrived to join its leisured set of the Michaelmas term of 1926. He was given a set of rooms handsome even by Canterbury Quad standards. Today they are still identified by the rubric Canterbury 3–3 and are still as spacious – for a start, four rooms rather than the usual two – but shared and shabby and anonymous, succeeding students leaving only a poster or a plastic cup or a fresh burn on the carpet as evidence of their occupancy.

Edward moved in in style. The dining room was hung with Flemish tapestries, the bedroom with crimson, grey and silver silk. A little extra room he had papered in a Napoleonic design of gold bees on a white ground, and the Oxford upholsterer who made the curtains was horrified at Edward's insistence they should reach the

floor and not merely the sills. The large drawing room – ah, the drawing room was given a purple ceiling and a frieze in gold lettering on black, ARS LONGA VITA BREVIS SED VITA LONGA SI SCIAS UTI which Edward rashly attributed to Seneca and which may be roughly translated as Art is long, life is short, but you can make life seem longer if you know how to use it.

Tom Driberg, a Christ Church contemporary (others included Christopher Sykes, Quintin Hogg, Valentine Dyall, Adam Black, Harry Oppenheimer, the present Duke of Montrose and, for one year only, W. H. Auden), remembered most vividly the 'latest French and American music belching from the mouths of busts of Roman emperors'. Betjeman, himself at Magdalen, celebrates in his poem the breakfasts of champagne and Virginia ham, the heady talk of Eliot and Wilde and Sachie's (Sacheverell Sitwell's) *Southern Baroque Art*, and each reciting to the other his latest poem while outside, in the rain, pale and uninteresting undergraduates trudged to lectures and tutorials.

This picture of perfumed indolence is not altogether complete. Reading History his first year under E. F. Jacob, a noted Mediaevalist, Edward satisfactorily passed History Prelim. In his second year he switched to Modern Languages with Frank Taylor, a New Zealander, as his tutor and every expectation of gaining a reasonable degree. He rode to hounds with the Bicester, buzzed up to London for the evening to see the ballet, edited the undergrad newspaper *Cherwell* with Betjeman and discovered an interest in printing. His closest friends were neither hearties nor aesthetes but social equals such as Basil Ava, heir to the Marquis of Dufferin, Lord Birkenhead's son Viscount Furneaux and – when he came up – Randolph Churchill. He had

From the entrance hall looking towards the library, in Mr and Mrs Willie's day. The polar bear Edward subsequently gave to Dali. Though overshadowed as a traveller by his brother Frank, Willie had been on Arctic expeditions as well as to Africa.

already met the Churchills through Professor Lindemann, who was a friend of his mother and a crony of Winston Churchill, destined to become the future war leader's scientific adviser. Edward remembers Lindemann telling him, as early as 1927, how atomic physics would lead one day to an atomic bomb.

But there is no doubt that he made his the most conspicuous wealth among a wealthy set. When Ava asked to borrow his car Edward *gave* it to him, and bought another. If you are looking for the most extravagant social change of Edward's lifetime it is not the decline of the great houses but the sheer unthinkability, these days, of a privileged class of gentlemen-commoners owing their place at university openly to wealth and snobbery. This is not to say that the comparably privileged do not exist; merely that they no longer advertise the fact. Classless blue denim and cheesecloth cover rich and poor alike. The rooms are uniformly dowdy. Even the view of the Dean's Garden that Edward enjoyed is now bisected by an anonymous new building.

Edward's first publishing venture was hatched at Oxford, a selection of John Betjeman's verse called *Mount Zion: or In Touch with the Infinite*. The second part of the title was an undergraduate joke mainly to support an illustration they'd found in a catalogue of a stout lady beatifically connected to a telephone, which Edward wanted to use as a frontispiece. It was Betjeman's first collection in print as well as Edition Number One from the James Press, as it was grandly termed, though from the grateful stanzas which the poet penned many years later and incorporated into *Summoned by Bells* it would seem that the slim volume didn't appear until after Betjeman had been sent down from Oxford and was pining away as a prep-school master in Gerrards Cross.

Edward's Oxford days were also coming to a close, but from nothing so dramatic as being sent down. Christ Church records indicate no more than that he was late back to college for the last two of the six terms he kept. His own explanation of his decision not to continue is that he enjoyed a reputation at Oxford for being brilliant but knew that he wouldn't be able to sustain it in his final exams. The clue to an alternative motive may be contained in the trip he made during one of the vacations. He went to Germany to see another friend and contemporary, Christopher Sykes (now the distinguished biographer), who had become an Honorary Attaché at the Embassy in Berlin. Harold Nicolson was Counsellor, and Edward stayed with him and Vita. He would soon come of age. Was he impatient to take his place in the world? And what more direct way of doing so than by playing at affairs of state himself?

FIVE

Edward went to Rome as an Honorary Attaché, which in a way was an extension of being a gentleman commoner at Christ Church. If you didn't actually pay for the privilege of being a gentleman-diplomat you certainly didn't receive a salary. On the other hand it was not done to be too ostentatious a spender and thus embarrass the career-diplomats. The first of three mistakes Edward made, he believes, was to arrive with a chauffeur-driven Rolls-Royce, though the Ambassador's displeasure (he was Sir Ronald Graham) did not inhibit him from deploying Edward, and the Rolls, and its chauffeur, if some distinguished visitor had to be met at the railway station. Edward also rented not one but two 14th century palaces in which to live, the Palazzo Celesia and the Palazzo Orsini, facing each other across the Tiber with a little island between and a bridge linking all three. Sometimes guests would be invited to take dinner in one palace and stroll across for coffee in the other, where a string quartet played.

The cook had come off the liner *Rex* and had to be discouraged from a taste that still ran to such scenic effects as lobster with eyes lit by electricity or an ice confection in the shape of the Victor Emmanuel Memorial. He also failed to take care of the crates of sugar which Edward had ordered from Fortnum and Mason before he left because his sister Sylvia had assured him, wrongly, that sugar was not to be found in Italy, so that rats got into it and one day Edward came home from his dipomacy to find the façade of the Orsini Palace whitened as by a miraculous snowfall. The cook had been tipping sugar into the street from an upper window, and lodging in the carvings and pinnacles it glistened in the sun. Rain came in the night to wash it away, but life was sweet enough already. For the hot summer Edward added a villa on the Aventine to his est.blishment. The Rolls was supplemented by a racy Alfa-Romeo. There was a companion he was evidently fond of, Francesco. One day they drove into the *campagna* and filled the car with baskets of wild narcissi bought cheap from a farmer, and remembering to give half of them to Lady Graham for the Embassy, Edward even managed to ingratiate himself there. Alas, two further contretemps with Sir Ronald lay in wait.

The first occurred while the Ambassador was away on leave. Edward was an animal-lover from childhood. He was upset by the narrow cages in which the live eagle and the live she-wolf, ancient emblems and mascots of Rome, were confined on Palatine Hill. He borrowed a sheet of ambassadorial writing paper to address a letter to the authorities pointing out what an unfortunate impression this gave visitors from England, and would it not be a truer reflection of Signor Mussolini's enlightened administration if the creatures could be given premises more like the Mappin Terraces in the London Zoo? Mr James would attend to any reply.

Edward was summoned to the Palazzo Venezia, at Mussolini's decree, he believes, but his youth disconcerted the officials who met him and the nearest he got to the dictator was an outer office. He said his piece and was politely rebuffed. Months later to his gratification it was announced that as a consequence of Il Duce's well-known humanity and love for all species new quarters were to be built for the wolf and the eagle. Unfortunately Sir Ronald found out about the letter.

The second incident was more serious, both by Foreign Service standards and as an early illustration of the petulance Edward has allowed to diminish so many of the activities to which he has brought his energy. He was on duty at the embassy one languid Sunday. Intelligence came in from a correspondent to the effect that against the provisions of the Locarno Treaty limiting naval construction, the keels of three warships appeared to have been laid down at La Spezia. It was Edward's task to encode the message and relay it to London. It was hot. The flies bothered him. The combination locks on the safe containing the code books eluded his skill until his fingers ached. Finally he got the safe open, whizzed off a signal and went home. In his hurry he converted three keels into three hundred, caused a flap in the Foreign Office and brought poor Ramsay MacDonald, the Prime Minister, hurrying back to Downing Street from Chequers. The Ambassador sent him on indefinite leave. His formal resignation took effect in October, 1930.

SIX

It wasn't the best of times for most people, as the frenzied twenties subsided into the depressed thirties, but London life, meaning the life of a favoured square mile or so in its centre, went on much as ever. In the grand town houses as many servants were kept as in Edwardian days. The débutante seasons continued unflaggingly. Rather opulent nightclubs opened. Young explorers off to Greenland or Spitsbergen danced their last evening away in the fashionable new May Fair Hotel. Edward, back from Rome, needed a London home and a base for all his activities.

He acquired the lease of 35, Wimpole Street, across from Number 50 where Elizabeth Barrett had been cooped up until rescued so romantically by Robert Browning – when Edward was ill for a spell once, he watched through his bedroom window the rebuilding of the Barrett house (it was being turned into flats), and saw exposed, before it was torn out, the very wallpaper that she must have stared and stared at, even the shadowy marks where her bed had been.

On the wrong side of Oxford Street, already a professional quarter with many of the properties occupied by doctors or dentists, it wasn't altogether the address that might have been expected from a wealthy young man about town. Mayfair was the accepted place. But Edward didn't see himself as a man about town. He loved going to the theatre, could never resist a party (and still can't); he was too much a product

Edward posed artistically in a down-the-stairwell interior of 35 Wimpole Street very much in the *Vogue* vogue of the day. If that's a telephone on the hall table, where is the flex? (*Norman Parkinson*)

of 'society' to be able to escape it; at the same time he longed to be a writer or artist or critic or editor on his own merits. He cultivated the company of working practitioners without realizing, at first, that they needed to work in order to eat. He tells the story against himself of how he was always hanging around Rex Whistler's studio in Fitzroy Square ('He was very poor, you know'), tremendously impressed by Whistler's refusal to answer the phone when he was working but unable to see that his presence was equally a distraction. The artist was too modest to tell him so, and in the end Oliver Messel had to take Edward aside and explain.

The likenesses of Edward which survive from his twenties, including that of the back of his head, twice over, in a famous Magritte painting, give an idea of how he looked: elegant profile save for a rather small jaw; dark hair with a slight wave, neatly but expensively shaped to the head; and the flawless complexion that is so often remembered. He was on the small side, but uniformly so – a very slightly scaled-down man. Ivan Moffat, Iris Tree's son and today a senior Hollywood screen writer, met him for the first time at one of Augustus John's parties down at Fordingbridge and retains a peculiarly vivid image of Edward about to leave again, driving himself for once, and at the wheel of a monstrous Mercedes sports car. It was his foot he noticed, 'a little foot on a powerful gas pedal'.

Edward dressed quietly, reserving – as at Oxford – his flamboyance for his surroundings. At Wimpole Street he had a dining-room carpet to a Rex Whistler design of Neptune surrounded by his court. He liked giving lunch parties for friends such as Iris Tree, the eccentric Lord Berners, Noël Coward, Edith Sitwell. He took on a butler, Thomas Pope, who stayed with him twenty years. He inherited a very good cellar from his mother. He avoided offending the matriarchs who supervised the social scene while acquiring some reputation for candour. 'The trouble with you, Edward,' boomed the formidable Lady Cunard, 'is that you will go around telling the truth. Now society is based upon a lie' – telling the story he imitates her with a protracted 'li-i-ie' – 'and if you persist you will not be received in decent houses!' He was also, by now, a very rich young man. On his 21st birthday he had come into a fortune left him by an uncle who died years before he was born, Frank Linsley James, the explorer and big game hunter killed by an elephant. When share prices began to recover from the stock market crash in America he would qualify for the epithet he much hated and always tried to disown, that of 'millionaire'. With the money, unfortunately but perhaps inevitably, came a growing belief that the rest of the world existed only to rob or cheat him of it. There was, for instance, the matter of his mother's house in the South of France.

She was now widowed a second time, and suffering from heart trouble. Edward visited her as often as he could, partly – he says – because no one else would. She had a knack of finding anyone's vulnerable spot and then needling away at it; she lost friends and found it hard to keep personal servants, a trait that some would say Edward has inherited. Their relationship was scratchy and, on her side, demanding. If he disagreed with her she accused him of being unkind – she would have another heart attack, and then he would be sorry. But he did feel sorry for her, between them lay some of the dependence on each other which can often link two people who seem

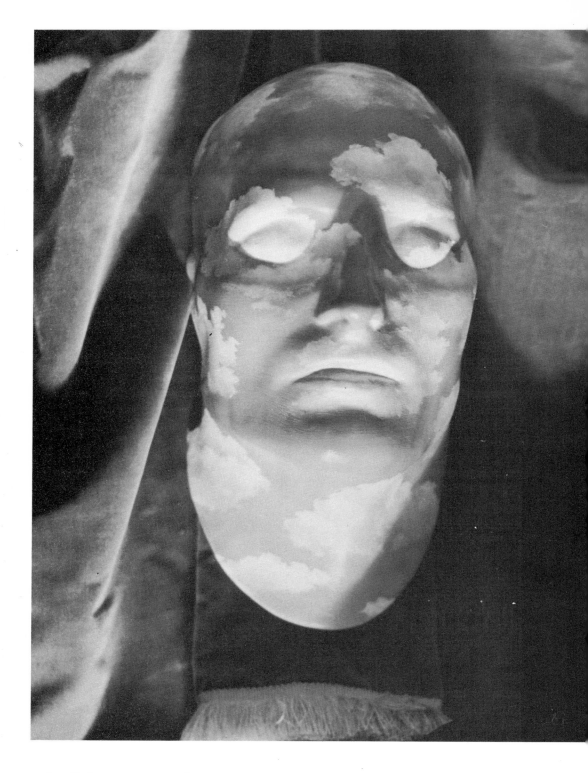

to be all their time quarrelling. She was spending more and more time in the South of France and when she asked him to build her a house there he readily agreed. The snag was that she wanted a level plot so that she could walk in the garden, while insisting on Roquebrune, where the land rose steeply from the sea. Edward was

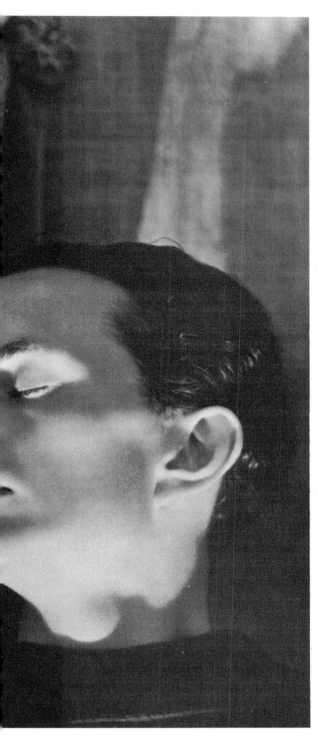

Edward with Napoleon death-mask decorated by Magritte. The curio has survived and figured in the Dada and Surrealist Exhibition at the Hayward Gallery, London, early in 1978. (*Norman Parkinson*)

forced to pay an extortionate price and in the end, he says, spent £100,000 on building a villa which before long he had to sell for a tenth of that sum, for scarcely had she moved in than poor Mrs Willie died.

This led to another famous grievance. His mother left debts which, rightly or

wrongly, the rest of the family expected Edward to shoulder alone – an imposition he later adapted for the hero of his novel *The Gardener Who Saw God*. Then there were suspicions of West Dean being let at far too low a rent, or of improvements to the house being authorized at unnecessarily high charges. Distrust began to poison

Another Wimpole Street
special: Edward at his
splendid desk, behind him an
even more splendid Picasso.
With a violinist friend.
(*Norman Parkinson*)

every activity, every new enthusiasm, into which Edward propelled himself. If he sent a picture to be cleaned the restorer was a zealot who ruined it. If he invited a composer into his house to write a great symphony, the composer and the composer's wife would be forever in Harrods ordering goodies on his account. If he

struck a deal with a painter to paint a fresco, the painter would eat his food and drink his drink but never complete the fresco. If he wanted to buy a house, word would somehow get around that he was who he was, and overnight the price would double. His cook in Rome in 1928 would be cheating him over the bills, and his cook in Hollywood twenty years later would be doing exactly the same. To this day, and unhappily with some reason, he remains convinced that the rich man's lot is, in the expressive catch-phrase of the moment, to be 'ripped off'.

There were a few satisfactory outlays, however. During his stay in Berlin with Christopher Sykes and the Nicolsons he had been enchanted by a picture he saw in a commercial gallery on the Unter den Linden, of birds against a landscape of forests

35 Wimpole Street today, about to reopen as the offices of a private medical organization, complete with parking meter. (*Robin Constable*)

and hills receding into the blue distance, full of the magic that he loved. It was a Jan Breughel, the twin of a better-known version hanging in the Palazzo Doria in Rome; and thanks to the runaway inflation of the German mark Edward was able to buy it, with an attestation from the director of the gallery, for a mere three hundred pounds. It was only because he couldn't find any more old masters at such prices, he sometimes professes, that he started to buy the works of young contemporary artists. They were still cheap.

His little publishing venture gave him no cause for discontent, either. He had bought shares in the Curwen Press in East London. Their typographer was David Garnett, the novelist, who seemed happy to pass on his expertise. After the Betjeman poems 'The James Press' brought out, in 1930, *Twenty Sonnets to Mary* by Edward himself, indeed ascribed simply to 'Edward'. The slender book is very elegant, with marbled boards, creamy paper, italic type. The poems, evidently written three years earlier to a girl (or boy) who otherwise seems to have left no enduring impression, are – well, just the sort of poems that any reasonably talented undergraduate of the period might have written during languid Oxford afternoons, stuffed with classical allusions and pastoral images.

> A jostling, swirling army of the air,
> has burst into these bosky, terraced glades,
> which earlier were tranquil as the shades
> of Proserpine's calm, whispering winter lair.

And so on and so on, fluent, facile and innocent of any real passion. Opus Three, dated 1931, is *Laengselia*, cautiously described as a play by Faustulus (*First draft*), in fact a whimsical version of Hans Andersen's *The Little Mermaid*, containing some mild satire on the social scene: a mermaid bright young thing says 'how stupendously delighted', another undersea character is dismissed as a social climber who 'would struggle to the surface of any sea *any* day if she thought it was going to promote her socially'. Requiring a full orchestra, a mezzo-soprano and a corps de ballet able to swim about the stage with graceful flicks of their tails, it was understandably never produced. Its sole interest lies in its provenance. Edward wrote it for the woman he married that year, and who cured him of his more ethereal notions of love.

SEVEN

Edward first set eyes on Tilly Losch in the Noël Coward revue *This Year of Grace* which C. B. Cochrane put on in 1928. There were two star dancers in it: Jessie Matthews, as English as can be, and Tilly, who was half Slavonic, half Jewish and

wholly Viennese. Edward was bowled over, particularly by her performance of a number called 'Gothic' in which she took up all the positions associated with 13th- and 14th-century sculpture, though perhaps not everyone in the audience would have appreciated this nicety. The music was Bach's 'Air on a G String'. 'Because I associated her with such beautiful music and beautiful sculpture', Edward now confides, 'I thought she must have a beautiful soul.' Well, he was only 21. He walked all round London trying to engineer an introduction, finally succeeding through an interior decorator who was doing some work for Tilly's mother.

Almost his first question to her was 'Did you devise the choreography yourself, Miss Losch?' She said, 'Yes, I did,' though Edward says he later discovered it was the work of her former partner Harald Krenzberg. Thus securely based on art rather than life, the courtship meandered on for the next two years. Once Edward climbed into her house in Curzon Street and she made it clear he could stay, but he was too shy, too naïve, he says, too full of romantic ideals. He did not sleep with her until they were married. He went to Rome, she to New York.

Of all the portraits of Tilly that survive the one that most captures her disturbing sexuality is the one made a few years on by Pavel Tchelitchew for the *Ballets 1933* programme. The huge, moody eyes gaze out from between high cheekbones – she had no trouble playing a Chinese in *The Good Earth* later still. The mouth is full, the chin like a little girl's – according to Edward, she would accent it lightly with rouge if she wanted to give herself a little-girl look. One elfin ear peeps out from thick hair hanging straight.

She was born in November 1904, making her two and a half years older than Edward, studied at the Court ballet school and joined the Vienna State Opera ballet in 1921. She was a soloist by 1924, as well as playing straight rôles at the Burgtheater. Max Reinhardt cast her in his *Midsummer Night's Dream* at Salzburg in 1927, for which she also did the choreography. C. B. Cochrane, ever on the lookout for popular stars amongst exponents of the higher arts, completed her transition to revue and musical comedy. She was very graceful, very feminine, very temperamental. She shared a dressing room with Jessie Matthews and they squabbled frequently as to whether the window should, or should not, be open. She was in another West End show, *Wake Up and Dream*, in 1929, then went to America.

Edward went to see her in New York early in 1931, and in the language of the light fiction of the day, popped the question. They were married within a week, on February 4th, at a church on Fifth Avenue. Edward lent the bride his car and went by taxi with his best man, Prince von Fuerstenberg – unfortunately, to the wrong church. Tilly, kept waiting, wasn't amused. She wore a rather everyday outfit of clipped lamb coat and matching hat which Edward decided, in retrospect, was chosen to indicate that no undue importance should be attached to the occasion. The guests nevertheless included Edward's immensely rich uncle (or, strictly, his cousin) Arthur Curtis James and his wife Harriet. The happy couple left first for Chicago, where Edward's sister Audrey – now married to the newspaper publisher Marshall Field – gave them dinner before they boarded the train for San Franscisco.

In the night Edward surprised Tilly by his ardour. 'You're rather a good lover,' she murmured, gratified. 'That makes something a little extra.' From his boyish looks and boyish manner, and – it should be conceded – his reticence before marriage, she had been quite convinced that like so many young men around the theatre he was queer. She remained half-convinced of it, or alternatively chose to revive the suspicion as soon as she tired of the marriage – she professed the belief that 'modern marriages need last only a few months', and when on the second day the train stopped at Reno, said, not absolutely in jest, 'Let's have the divorce now.'

Even the honeymoon in Hawaii was the occasion for subsequent recriminations. There was this beach-boy Edward kept photographing and whom she once found in their room. Edward, it must be admitted, has an extraordinary knack of putting himself in the worst possible light as he brings up these stories, protesting just a shade too vehemently, elaborating just a shade too plausibly. He did take a lot of photographs of the boy, because he was such a beautiful human being, but the one time he came into their room was to help Edward close his trunk the day they were leaving. Whether someone is heterosexual, homosexual or bisexual is these days of less

Tilly in front of somewhat sentimental
group of the Losch family, flanked by
Mutti and Hitlerian Papa. The young
Tilly is immediately behind her
grown-up self. (*Radio Times Hulton
Picture Library*)

On the honeymoon: Tilly's owlish
sun-glasses suggest that she wasn't
expecting a photographer to drop by.

account. The matter is raised simply in the context of Tilly's accusations; while it is raised, it might as well be settled. Edward freely admits to homophile leanings at various times in his life: he has been in love with men as well as with women. There is a sequence of sonnets he wrote sometime in the mid-forties invoking a journey with a loved one from Oregon down through California and Arizona to the Mexican border; one line reveals that the companion is a man. Another attachment mellowed into a friendship that has lasted thirty years. In Hollywood he moved a good deal in gay circles and was once arrested by, he says, an *agent provocateur* from the Vice Squad who fortunately couldn't make the charge stick. But he insists that he never wanted to consummate a relationship with another man. He likes women too much.

Certainly he was passionately in love with Tilly, and while it lasted the honeymoon had its sweetnesses. Edward wrote three Hawaiian lyrics though also a touching poem *To Ottilie* (Ottilie Ethel Losch being her full name) likening their relationship to a mirage seen in the desert, a distant sea with a sail upon it:

> I your one lover, you my wife
> Until we dissolve and are
> Just as that mirage seen from far,
> A sudden sparkle on a sea
> Which is, yet only seems to be.

On the way back they stopped off in Palm Springs to see a friend and fellow Austrian of Tilly's, Count Friedrich Ledebur. He was – is – a giant of a man, who later married Iris Tree and later still became a film actor, most famously as Queequeg in *Moby Dick*. Tilly told Edward, 'You must meet him. He's so big and jolly', and curiously the two men did get on very well together despite a difference in height of over a foot; but only a few months later Edward found that Tilly had been citing Ledebur as representative of the raffish Bohemian set into whose company her husband had drifted.

This was back in New York. Edward had taken an apartment on 57th Street. It was the late summer of 1931. The Churchills were all installed at the Waldorf Towers at the start of a lecture tour by Winston. From them Edward learned that the National Government which had succeeded Labour planned to take Britain off the gold standard. He sailed on the *Bremen*, spent three hectic days in London transferring assets that would be affected and caught the same liner back after its turn-around in Germany. His sister Audrey greeted him with the news that his little wife had been to see them, very upset because of the company he was keeping.

Edward had hoped to take Tilly back to England for the summer but unbeknown to him, he claims, she had signed up for the musical *The Band Wagon*. Edward went to the opening in Philadelphia. Helen Broderick, a tough old Broadway actress in the cast, took one look at him and said to Tilly, 'Does your husband travel half fare?' He was in fact twenty-three but was this part of the trouble? – a beautiful woman already fearing the day when the bloom of youth would fade, and married to a husband not only her junior in years (more years than she would ever admit, says Edward uncharitably) but one who looked absurdly younger still. Or was it simply the impossibility of two such total egocentrics ever accommodating to each other? Tilly was a model of the ambitious performer for whom career always comes first. When she found she was pregnant and told him she was going to have an abortion, because of the show, Edward objected that it might prevent children in the future. He still imitates the coldness with which she snapped back, 'Don't be silly!'

Edward, for his part, could hardly have been worse prepared by upbringing for the give and take of marriage. His father had died when he was five, his mother-figure had been chased away. His youngest sister was seven years older. He was spoiled, and yet deprived, generous yet wary, full of romantic notions about the fusion of souls but blind to the practical need to adjust attitudes. In his many stories of life with Tilly, recalled in painful detail, he never says 'us' or 'we' or 'our'. It is always my house, my child, my friends, Tilly's friends.

For the time being the marriage zig-zagged along with occasional raptures and rather more tantrums. To occupy himself during the run of *The Band Wagon* Edward learned to fly and bought a private plane, a Stinson. With it he first visited the Mexican border that was so to attract him in later years. Finally he was able to take his wife to England and the ancestral home.

EIGHT

Wimpole Street was being refurbished to flatter Tilly, with an alabaster bathroom for her designed by Paul Nash and a white-on-white bedroom designed by Edward himself, in the first of a series of ever more extravagant attempts to please her. In the meantime they moved into a little house at 3 Culross Street, off Grosvenor Square, which Edward had bought for just such an eventuality. While they were in America he'd lent it to Randolph Churchill, who kept his latch-key and would sometimes drop in on them in the middle of the night. Perhaps for this reason, perhaps because a proper W.1 address appealed to Tilly's sense of values, she was always happiest there. West Dean, to which Edward had at last succeeded, and with which he most desired to impress his wife, never attracted her much. She spent only long enough there for Edward to conceive his romantic gesture of having her wet footprint immortalized in Axminster carpet. Large staffs would be taken on, vast cleanings and airings carried out, then no one would arrive.

There were jolly holidays. Edward had his aeroplane and also a yacht in the Mediterranean. He ordered from the coachbuilders a special Rolls-Royce, copied from Lord Louis Mountbatten's, in which the seats folded down to make a bed. It was meant again for Tilly, but he was to be the one that mostly used it, driven

How *The Tatler* rose to the revival of *The Miracle* at the Lyceum. Note that in those days even a temperamental man of the theatre like Max Reinhardt always wore a respectable suit, collar and tie. (*Mander & Mitchenson*)

down to West Dean in the small hours by his faithful chauffeur and left there, parked under the porch, snoozing away in clean pyjamas between clean sheets, until his equally faithful butler woke him at 10 a.m. with orange juice and coffee.

Edward hankered to please his wife most of all by furnishing her with an artistic triumph in the theatre. His *Little Mermaid* script could perhaps become more of an operetta, even a ballet. He actually commissioned a score from Georges Auric, but Auric never delivered it. Instead, Tilly went into a revival of *The Miracle*, a perfervid religious spectacle which had enjoyed a great vogue before the First World War. The story came from mediaeval legend and concerned a nun who leaves her devotions to go into the forest with her lover. A statue of the Madonna comes to life, takes her place and bears her punishment for her. The book was by von Hoffmansthal, the music by Humperdinck, but it was chiefly an opportunity for the great master of stage *schmalz*, Max Reinhardt, to achieve his effects. As before, Cochrane presented the production, the auditorium of the Lyceum Theatre (a dance hall since the Second World War) being given some Gothic arches over the boxes to impart a cathedral-like air; the society beauty Lady Diana Manners (later Cooper) portrayed the Madonna, and was always the favourite of a society audience.

Tilly, of course, was the nun, and it is possible that she did not relish playing second fiddle to an amateur, especially when the amateur's mother, the Duchess of Rutland, would come to rehearsals and hoot to Reinhardt or his assistant, 'Not enough light on my daughter; too much on Miss Losch.' A high moment in the show came when the nun discarded her veil and escaped into the forest with her knight, whereupon the Madonna came to life in nine graceful movements, gathered up the veil with one more and let it float into place over her head. At rehearsals it always went beautifully. On the first night Edward was surprised to see Tilly tie a knot in the veil before she let it flutter to the ground. The Madonna, foxed, had to add a couple of less graceful movements before she could don it. At the celebration afterwards a chill silence greeted Tilly, but such was her magic, when she chose to turn it on, that by the end of the party she had charmed everyone, except perhaps Lady Diana, into forgiveness. Later in the run, the Madonna summoned Edward to her dressing room, bared her shoulder to reveal a cluster of flea-bites and said, 'Look what your darling wife has done now', but Edward generously believes that they were none of Tilly's doing, it was just an old theatre.

The revival failed to repeat the success of the original 1911 production, at least in London, though Lady Diana subsequently toured with it round Europe and America. Tilly felt that whatever she wanted in life was slipping away again, and flitted back to New York, ostensibly to see about a part in a new musical, in reality – says Edward – to look up an old lover, Sergé Obolensky, an émigré Russian prince who was married to Alice Astor, acted as public relations adviser to a number of hotel chains and had lately become a United States citizen. According to Edward again, she was trying to persuade him to leave his wife and marry her as soon as they could both obtain divorces. Edward himself went to the South of France to conclude the sale of his mother's house, and there fell into the arms of a married woman several years older than himself. Edward had three important affairs (important to him, anyway)

"THE MIRACLE" REVIVAL AT THE LYCEUM

MAX REINHARDT REHEARSING MISS TILLY LOSCH

(Right) AND
MAX STILL
WITH HIS
EYE ON THE
REHEARSAL

MR. OLIVER MESSEL, MISS TILLY LOSCH (back to camera), AND LADY DIANA COOPER

For the Cochran-Reinhardt production of "The Miracle," which opens at the Lyceum between April 4th and 6th, the theatre has undergone most elaborate preparations. The idea is to make the audience feel they are in a cathedral; therefore the front of the stage and the boxes are covered with a framework of Gothic tracery, and it all looks very solid and imposing. The orchestra and an organ are installed in the gallery. Where the orchestra usually is has become a crypt beneath the stage, and characters will enter this way. Lady Diana Cooper is again playing the part of the Madonna, and Miss Tilly Losch is, admittedly, the Nun. All these pictures were taken during rehearsals at which Max Reinhardt, one of the world's great producers, presided in person

PROFESSOR NILSON (the Musical Director) AND
MISS TILLY LOSCH

during the next few years. He scrupulously avoids naming the ladies while letting slip so much circumstantial detail that identification is not difficult. Since two of them are still very much alive, however, as is the husband of the third, good manners invite our discretion.

This liaison was particularly important. Not only did the Frenchwoman restore his confidence in himself and do something towards healing the wounds that Tilly

Tilly the star: a picture for her fans.
(*Mander & Mitchenson*)

had made, she introduced him into circles which were to have a profound effect on his future. Through her he became a friend of the Aldous Huxleys, along the coast at Sanary. Admiration of a portrait of the lady by a relatively unknown Spanish painter led to his interest in, and eventual friendship with, Salvador Dali. More immediately, she took him to Paris and involved him in the hopes and plans of a group of artists working in the ballet. With the death of Diaghilev the Russian Ballet which had astonished and delighted Europe throughout the twenties had divided into two factions, one led by Leonid Massine, the other by Georges Balanchine and Boris Kochno. Balanchine had formed a small company of ten dancers, and was looking for financial support. Would Edward chip in say £2,000, along with Edith Chanel and the Polignacs and the de Noailles and everyone?

Edward went along to a rehearsal and was excited. The company was working on a new ballet, *Mozartiana*, to music actually by Tchaikowsky from a Mozart theme, and with décor by Christian Berard. Other ballets were commissioned from contemporary composers and designers, awaiting only the means to go ahead. Edward threw himself into the venture. It was something in which he could invest ideas and inspiration as well as more and more money. Above all, by attaching to the investment the trifling condition that Tilly be invited to join the company, he secured the perfect opportunity of giving her the triumph she craved. Tilly rose to the bait. Edward set out, in the words of Patrick Boyle in the best of the few magazine articles to have appeared about him (*Telegraph* Sunday Magazine, May 1977), to make 'one of the most grandiose bids a rich man ever made to recapture the wife he loved'.

NINE

Under Edward's largesse, and to suit his dreams, *Les Ballets 1933* expanded in aim from a single programme to a repertory of ballets from which any three might be performed on a given evening. The name of M. Edward James figured prominently in the brochure that was being designed. He also contributed a preface in sonorous French proclaiming that, as the title suggested, the ballets were very much of the moment; they represented no new theory or school of dance; they were the fruits of instinctive necessity. Instinctive necessity had included, in Edward's case, the necessity to accommodate Tilly in a company which already included an assured prima ballerina, Tamara Toumanova.

Toumanova would dance *Mozartiana*, also *Les Songes* to music by Darius Milhaud and designs by André Derain, and *Fastes*, same designer, music by Henri Sauguet. Assuming that Tilly would not be as technically proficient, Balanchine and Kochno suggested that she should be given a ballet which did not require any sustained points

In spikey costume in *Wake Up and Dream* at the
London Pavilion, 1929; other dancer is Toni
Birkmayr. (*Radio Times Hulton Picture Library*)

work. Edward proposed they should approach Pavel Tchelitchew, the Russian painter and scene designer he had known and admired since Edith Sitwell introduced them in London in 1929. The resulting ballet, which in fact was Tchelitchew's entire concept, was *L'Errante*, to Schubert's 'Wanderer' Sonata as orchestrated by Koecklin; the dancer, searching for love and companionship through dream-like encounters, was required mainly to run around ahead of an enormous flowing green train. Edith Sitwell came to a performance and declared that she could see in the swirling garment the green of forests, the green of water.

Tilly had meanwhile demonstrated, in no uncertain fashion, that she was as classically competent as anyone. *Les Valses de Beethoven* was added, which used some Beethoven tunes orchestrated by Nicholas Nabokov (cousin of the writer Vladimir Nabokov) for a perfectly classical ballet of Apollo and Daphne. It was the sixth ballet and third vehicle for Tilly that owed most to Edward's own inspiration, proved to be the most controversial item of the season and is certainly the most enduring work to emerge from it. Edward's idea was to represent the divided nature of woman by having two dancers, one embodying the grasping, practical side, the other the romantic, passionate side. How much it derived from marriage with Tilly is anyone's guess. He wrote out a scenario and asked Kurt Weill, composer of *The Threepenny Opera* and *Maha Gonny* if he would write the music. Weill was interested but proposed using a singer instead of one dancer, with his usual collaborator Bertolt Brecht furnishing the poems ('lyrics' was hardly a word you used with Brecht) and their favourite interpreter Lotte Lenya – who was also Weill's wife – coming in to sing them. And they would get the designer who had done *Dreigroschenoper* in Germany, Caspard Neher.

Brecht was summoned from Berlin, which was lucky timing for him, because soon after Hitler came to power and had he stayed he might well have been arrested in one of the first round-ups of known Communists. At first he refused the commission on the grounds that he was unwilling to work for a Wall Street capitalist who fancied he could dabble in the arts but, swayed by Weill, relented. Preparations went on all through the winter of 1932–33. For a while the whole circus moved over to London and Edward put up composers, designers, hangers-on.

A sadder prelude to the venture is recorded in *The Next Volume*, which was indeed the next volume from the James Press, containing Edward's Hawaiian poems and decorations by Rex Whistler. The book is dated 1932 but a correction slip reads, 'Publication of this book was withheld until January 1933 owing to the serious illness of the author's wife.' Tilly had become pregnant by Edward again and this time, ironically, seemed content to have the baby – how it would all be fitted into the programme of preparations and rehearsals that lay ahead was something neither of them seemed to have considered very much. But at a late stage she started to haemorrhage and the doctors advised Edward that she might be in danger if they didn't bring the birth on. The boy (it would have been) did not live.

Les Ballets 1933 opened at the Théâtre des Champs Elysées in the summer, played there for three months and then moved to the Savoy Theatre, London, meeting with critical success in both cities. Though purists were disconcerted by its mixture of

Cartoon of Tilly as the Nun in *The Miracle*, from *The Sketch*, July 1928. (*Mander & Mitchenson*)

song, dance and speech – and especially the idea that a dancer (Tilly) should speak – the greatest acclaim was for the 'Spectacle sur des poèmes de Bert Brecht' called at the time *Anna, Anna* (reflecting the duality of the heroine) but best known today by the title under which it survives in the concert hall as well as the theatre, *The Seven Deadly Sins*.

L'Errante was also well received, despite its fair share of mishaps. Tchelitchew's décor, it was discovered at the last minute, couldn't be fire-proofed to meet the Lord Chamberlain's very strict regulations in London. The artist had to design and execute a new set in nine hours. Then, during one of the performances another dancer trod on Tilly's fifteen-foot train and tore it. Tilly signalled to the corps de ballet to improvise, shot off stage and up the spiral staircase to her dressing room and was back in her rehearsal costume within three minutes. *L'Errante* was subsequently performed in America, and revived again after the war, by Lincoln Kerstein, to whom Edward assigned such rights as he had in the ballets – a matter not always very clear: Bert Brecht turned up on the stage in Copenhagen once to stop a performance of *Anna, Anna*.

Whether the season could be regarded as a popular success is a matter of disagreement. According to a letter from Tchelitchew to friends in Paris the London run, at least, was a fiasco. They could not fill even a small theatre compared with the theatres Diaghilev had filled. According to Edward it was full houses every night. But in compliance with the eternal law (or lore) of James, there was certainly no profit in the venture for the man who put up all the money. His rôle, as usual, was to pay out. The takings vanished into the costs of renting the theatres, transporting the scenery, engaging a full symphony orchestra and rewarding the cluster of talents he had drawn into the show. It cost him nearly £100,000. And it failed to save his marriage.

TEN

The divorce was ugly. Another couple, if unable to avoid it altogether, would at least have arranged for a discreet parting of the ways. With Tilly and Edward, unfortunately, it was a case of irresistible bloody-mindedness up against immovable obstinacy. The final collision was precipitated, rather symbolically, by the party Edward planned for the *Les Ballets* company at the end of the London run. Tilly was living at Culross Street under an agreement giving her tenure of the little house as long as she refrained from further demands. Edward wanted the piano back for his party at Wimpole Street. There was a fearful row. Tilly brought an action for a separation allowance on the grounds of his cruelty and his homosexuality. Edward countered with a divorce suit, on grounds of her infidelity, which was considered

Lady Diana as The Madonna. Her outfit was designed by Oliver Messel to assist her in keeping an absolutely statuesque stillness for the first half of the spectacle, and was a cross between a costume and a plaster cast. (*Mander & Mitchenson*)

unsporting by man-about-town standards; you were supposed to allow the little woman to be the innocent party. Tilly chose to defend the suit, which was madness by any standards: the dirt came tumbling out, all reportable in the papers.

Obolensky was cited as co-respondent. All sorts of luminaries found themselves in the witness box, from Sir Thomas Beecham to Randolph Churchill and Tom Mitford, brother of Nancy and Jessica and Diana and Unity. Tilly had Sir Patrick Hastings, Q.C., as Counsel, Edward had the younger, then less eminent Norman Birkett (later Lord Birkett) who had no great difficulty in puncturing some of Tilly's more lurid romances. Proceedings lasted eight days, at the end of which Edward was granted his decree nisi but none of his friends would speak to him.

The rancour with which Edward recalls the marriage, the light he puts upon almost every one of Tilly's actions, the accusations he makes, aren't pretty: she only married him for his money, anticipating a straightforward little annulment and handsome settlement as soon as she could discover, to her shock and dismay, that he was a homosexual; thwarted, she went out to prove it anyway; en route she seduced his best friends; she refused to bear his children; even the last miscarriage was doubtless the consequence of quinine she had taken earlier to try and terminate the pregnancy. Then suddenly the rancour and the resentment are directed at associates and hangers-on who stayed under his roof and ate his food and drank his wine while Tilly was in hospital but sent not even a bunch of violets; and just as nuclear physicists track invisible particles by their impact on other matter, you glimpse for an instant the hollow left by aching love.

If Tilly had ever completed the autobiography she began, perhaps the story could be revised sharply in her favour. Lord Weidenfeld, the publisher, and her neighbour in Eaton Place in the sixties, saw a first chapter once. She began with the loss of that baby. Meanwhile it has to be admitted that she displayed no subsequent talent for marriage. After another Cochrane revue, *Streamline* in 1934, she went to Hollywood to make *The Garden of Allah* and *The Good Earth*, in which she played the adulteress. In 1939 she married the Earl of Carnarvon, but stayed with him – it was said – only ten weeks before sailing to America once again. The marriage was dissolved in 1947; at the Earl's insistence Tilly continued to style herself 'Countess of Carnarvon'. Sergé Obolensky, a man of great charm and dash who had fought in the Czarist Russian army in the First World War, enlisted in the American army in the Second and although nearly fifty became a parachutist, once dropping in literally on English friends in Northamptonshire. As for Edward . . . in a poem written ten or twelve years later he was still trying to exorcise a ghost. Is it Tilly?

> *I do at moments think about her yet –*
> explain to me how one so like a child
> could be so cruel, should be so false, so wild.
> Believe me this: – she spun a kind of net
> like some weird, magic spider with her charm
> about more men than me.
>
>   She still may harm
> my peace, unless you teach me to forget.

Yes, she was young; but, as one in a tower
surveys the world, detached. She loved a storm
and leaned towards the lightning to perform
dark rites; but pouted like a child when sour.
You want to pierce the nature of her power,
her face, her character, her tone, her form.
Now, understand, she was not kind, nor warm;
and you do for me daily in one hour
more loving, gentle things than she in all
the months she knew me ever did. The sum
of every sweetness she accorded then
would never total half which I recall
you gave me yesterday.
      My darling, come
let us not ever mention her again.

At the time of writing the two ex-husbands and the lover are all alive. Tilly died in 1975. Her last film rôle of note was as the Mexican woman, Mrs Chavez, in that torrid Western *Duel in the Sun*. Later she introduced a television show sponsored by General Motors. She took up painting in the naïve manner, held one or two exhibitions ('a pleasant Sunday painter', said *The Times*) and settled for the last time in London.

ELEVEN

Exhausted and drained of emotion, Edward withdrew to West Dean and lived there, mostly alone, for a year. He had always been interested in growing things. He busied himself with the affairs of the garden. And one evening in the spring of 1935 he experienced an extraordinary vision or hallucination, whichever way you account for these things. He was eating his solitary dinner. Suddenly the dining-room ceiling seemed to part, and to the music of Beethoven's *Eroica* he saw a great swirling vision of the creation of the world. He was so overcome he had to leave the table and go into another room, where presently his puzzled butler found him.

The whole phenomenon lasted some ten or fifteen minutes. Edward has no doubt it was subjective, but bursting to record the experience he found himself casting it in the form of a novel, ascribing it to someone for whom it was utterly real. *The Gardener Who Saw God* is almost the only book of Edward's to enjoy normal commercial publication (by Duckworth). Indeed it ran into a second edition, and an American edition. It also by far his best prose work, one of those lone novels (like Eugène Fromentin's *Dominique*) with a sharp individuality which the author never

Messel also drew this very charming sketch of Tilly as a shepherdess. (*Edward James Foundation*)

Tilly's footprints woven into staircarpet at West
Dean House in shades of green. (*Robin Constable*)

attempts again. It is so very nearly very good that its digressions and irrelevancies and knowing asides and little bits of moralizing are all the more irritating.

The story opens with another incident which Edward resourcefully took from recent first-hand experience – driving up to the Chelsea Flower Show with a collection of orchids and lilies, being unable to display them to full advantage because the proper staging hasn't arrived, and having to be content with second prize instead of first. The detail is so vivid that the reader is drawn into the hopes and fears of the hero, supposedly a humble gardener called Joseph Smith, despite a gathering certainty that the author knows very little about humble persons of any calling.

Joseph is gentle, conscientious, uncommunicative. He has been subjected to the same injustice which Edward encountered, only scaled down to hundreds of pounds rather than tens of thousands, of being obliged to settle his late mother's debts while four elder siblings pocket their share of the estate. He has suffered from the rejections of a calculating Irish girl who has some of the attributes of Tilly. He has also been married to an idealized girl who died young, which may represent the philosophy made fashionable in the plays of Jean Anouilh a few years later, that death is the only true way of keeping love alive. He is endowed by the author with an instinctive appreciation of art and music.

There are also plenty of above-the-stairs characters drawn sardonically from the world more familiar to Edward. Mrs Deathon Astring was based on Lady Colefax, the interior designer, Lady Judas Iscariot on Lady Juliet Duff, Lady Marionette on Nancy Cunard – but there are references to Lady Cunard under her own name as well, as a bit of clever double-bluff. An eccentric Lord Bullborough who has giant ears built on to his house and a grand piano in a tree is clearly inspired by the real-life eccentric and friend of Edward's, Gerald Berners, who built a famous folly on his estate at Faringdon and dyed his tame pigeons pretty colours.

There is a tiresome surrealist poet who is given a whole chapter in which to expound the surrealist creed to a bemused Joseph, and a pretty girl in the swimming pool who turns out, perhaps significantly, perhaps not, to have been born the same year as Edward James and have the same rather clouded paternity. It is altogether such a ragbag of different stuffs that it shouldn't have any cohesion, yet in some strange way it does. Towards the end the narrative returns to the starting point, and Joseph's mood at the end of the long day following the flower show disappointment. He has travelled back to the big house (which Edward modelled not on West Dean but on Castle Howard in Yorkshire) with the old housekeeper Mrs Magginery, the one really splendid characterization in the book. What follows is related in a sustained, strange, haunting hundred or more pages. The family is away. Drawn to the library Joseph studies the absent master's books and pictures, plays his records on his gramophone. A carved figure brought back from Spain crashes mysteriously to the floor. Upstairs in her room old Mrs Magginery suffers a heart attack and, all alone, grumbling to herself, dies. The clock ticks away the hours. Joseph at last goes back to his cottage, drinks some red wine (he is a gardener of eclectic tastes), and wanders out again into the hushed night garden.

Tchelitchew's jacket design for *The Gardener Who Saw God* depicts the hero in mid-vision. (*Robin Constable*)

Then in the lower part of the sky, towards the horizon to the left of the elms, very imminent he saw taking colour as well as form and gaining in precision, flocks and flocks of those small white spring gladioli with butterfly markings that are named Nymph gladioli . . . rapidly, kaleidoscopically, as if by a big wind the formation of the cloud-built flowers became puffed into larger and larger contours. And now they were no longer clouds at all, but real petals of moist and breathing flowers filling the entire heaven . . .

The vision proceeds in a great set piece, from botanic to zoological to apocalyptic images, all swirling and whirling in the sky, until:

Joseph dared no longer look up. Something was going to explode above . . . He did not see the sudden flash or hear the roar that came: he felt them: he received a heavy physical blow upon his head and shoulders and fell for a moment senseless to the ground.

TWELVE

When it was published two years later *The Gardener* attracted glowing reviews from Richard Church, Howard Spring, Harold Brighouse, Frank Swinnerton and *Country Life* ('There is a description of the Royal Horticultural Show which alone would make the book worth reading'), and one by James Agate from which the publishers could at least extract a favourable quote for the second-edition wrapper. The cover design of Joseph squinting up at the gathering vision out of the corner of his eye, as if not daring to turn full face to it, was by Tchelitchew.

Edward and he had remained friends since the ballets. Pavel Tchelitchew (sometimes spelt with a final *-ff* instead) was a Russian aristocrat who fled the aftermath of the Revolution, joined a travelling theatre in Turkey as scene-painter in exchange for bed and board, and eventually landed up in Paris among all the other starving artists. He was discovered by Gertrude Stein and through her became friendly with Edith Sitwell, subject of half-a-dozen of his best-known portraits and also of a wax head, one of his very few sculptures. The portrait which is in the Tate Gallery is Edward's. Another belongs to Edith's brother, Sir Sacheverell Sitwell. The extraordinary profile is set as squarely against a rich, Renaissance-like background as in a Piero della Francesca likeness of a Florentine worthy. Yet from the same period Edward owns a Tchelitchew modishly assembled entirely from sequins. He was also a remarkable draughtsman. A later portrait head hanging in Edward's home in Mexico is made up of fine concentric lines, like contours on an infinitely detailed map, and all done freehand.

He was an exuberant character, going from sudden rages to high spirits, very generous, very considerate. He arrived at West Dean towards the end of Edward's

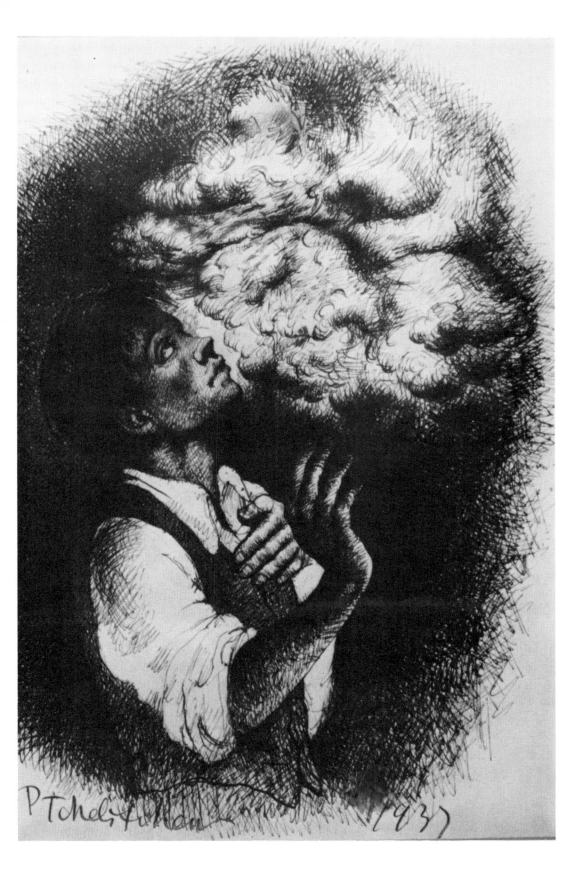

The grounds of the Villa Cimbrone at Ravello which
Edward rented from Lord Grimthorpe every summer. His
lordship was peeved when Edward's newspaper story
about Garbo and Stokowski brought the villa unwelcome
(to him) publicity. (*Mansell Collection*)

year of rustication and did much to cheer him up. There was a plan which never
came to anything for him to paint a fresco round the great staircase. Tchelitchew was
far from being a surrealist artist but he brought with him the companion of his
later years, the young American poet Charles Henri Ford, who pursued the surrealist
aim of random juxtapositions, opening the dictionary at hazard, picking a word,
opening it again. 'Why don't you do the same, Edward?' Tchelitchew would
tactlessly bray. 'You'll never get anywhere while you're so conservative.' Edward
typed out Keats's *Ode to a Nightingale* and tried that on him, but the painter refused
to see either virtue in the poem or irony in the gesture. Even when, much later,
Edward had just bought eight of his pictures from a gallery in Rome, Tchelitchew
harangued him about his true talent in life being that of a collector, on which he
should henceforth concentrate all his energy, e.g. by buying yet more Tchelitchews.

Charles Henri, says Edward, put his head close to the artist's and murmured, 'Pavel, je crois que tu fais des gaffes.' Despite misunderstanding and quarrels of various kinds over the years, plus the inevitable suspicion on Edward's part sooner or later that the artist was trying to overcharge his patron, they remained friends until Tchelitchew's death in 1957.

Edward emerged from his seclusion. The complicated business of enjoying life had to be resumed. He flew his aeroplane down to Cap Ferrat to see Syrie Maugham and was arrested for landing on the beach without bothering about customs formalities. He sailed his yacht round the coast of Spain and through the Greek islands. He took Edith Sitwell on a motor tour of Italy, with a special detour to the sea-coast where Shelley drowned. He found a villa, the Villa Cimbrone at Ravello, above Amalfi, where he was so happy that he agreed to rent it for seven years, an arrangement cut short only by the outbreak of war. And he embarked upon the second of his three post-Tilly love affairs. She was a young German dancer from the Monte Carlo ballet whom Edward tried to groom for stardom by dressing her expensively at Schiaparelli, and who in fact did become a film actress and is these days married to an American television executive. Edward and she still correspond.

When they travelled together and he introduced her to acquaintances, Edward was amused because she would always go out of her way to mention her mother ('My mother who is with us, you know') as if this made the *ménage* respectable. Mother, as it happened, was a keen Nazi and the mistress of Hans Thomsen, the Foreign Ministry official who crops up in many memoirs of this period and who became the Reich's last Charge d'affaires in Washington. Edward went to the 1936 Olympic Games in Berlin with them. The romance, as he ironically prefers to term the affair (with an odd short 'o') ended when Mutti demanded that Edward either marry her daughter or affix his signature to a large cheque.

A graver sign of the times to mar the round of pleasure was an empty place as Edward's guests gathered at Ravello that same summer: among those invited had been the poet Federico Garcia Lorca, murdered in the first days of the Spanish Civil War.

THIRTEEN

Edward's involvement with art and artists of this period is conveniently summed up by *Minotaure*, an avant-garde magazine of the arts with which he was associated. It was produced by the Paris publisher Albert Skira, who was also issuing a series of reproductions of French paintings. Edward put money into both projects and in the end, inevitably, fell out with Skira, but the earlier *Minotaures*, at all events, show his influence. The very first issue devoted two pages to a facsimile of Kurt Weill's

Edward's close friend for many years was the eccentric
peer, and gifted musician, Gerald Berners, seen here
with Gertrude Stein. (*Radio Times Hulton Picture
Library*)

As a schoolboy Edward had fallen under the spell of the 'stormy petrels' of the cultural scene, Osbert, Edith and Sacheverell Sitwell and their poetry magazine *Wheels*. He became most friendly with Edith, seen here with Osbert. (*Radio Times Hulton Picture Library*)

Anna, Anna score, then newly composed. His favourite artists, Tchelitchew and Dali, designed covers and title pages, as did Picasso. His own contributions included poems (in French) with drawings by Dali and a mock-learned dissertation (also in French) on Queen Mary's formidable hats. Though publication was supposed to be quarterly it was in practice sporadic; in all there were thirteen issues between 1933 and 1939, the last two bound together as a double number.

It wasn't all modernism. Edward also contributed a piece in English, *The Marvel of Minuteness*, in praise of 16th-century portrait miniatures he had come across in Vienna. Someone else wrote about the Pre-Raphaelites. The camera reportage of Bill Brandt was represented. But the true predilection of the editorial policy was

implicit in the interests declared on the mast-head: 'Arts Plastiques, Poésie, Musique, Architecture, Ethnologie, Mythologie, Spectacles, Psychologie, Psychiatrie, Psychanalyse', give or take a couple of items, the hobby-horses of the Surrealists.

Surrealism didn't just happen. It was formulated quite deliberately, out of the debris of several wild and woolly art movements, notably the nihilist Dada group whose more famous exploits had included a reproduction of the Mona Lisa decorated with a moustache and supplied with an obscene caption, and the Cologne exhibition of 1920 at which visitors were invited to smash the exhibits with a chopper, helpfully

provided. It also owed much to fashionable theories of psychology emanating from
Freud. The *Manifesto of Surrealism*, published in 1924 by André Breton, founder and
leader of the movement, decried the rationalism and logic which ruled the world
and urged instead that fantasy, superstition and the unconscious mind be explored
in the search for truth. Surrealism, in a famous if grim definition that followed, was
'Pure psychic AUTOMATISM, by which it is intended to express verbally, in
writing or in any other way, the true process of thought. It is the dictation of thought,
free from the exercise of reason and every aesthetic or moral preoccupation'.

In practice, automatism proved rather difficult to engineer, especially in painting.
Writers could plonk down stream–of–consciousness prose or the kind of poem
Tchelitchew recommended to Edward. Works of art could be 'found' by signing a
bicycle wheel, filling a bird–cage with lumps of sugar or arranging a pile of bricks, a
tradition which survives today. But how could the act of putting paint on canvas be
freed from conscious design? Max Ernst devised a technique of *frottage*, whereby he
took rubbings of surfaces that appealed to him and transferred them to his canvas.
André Masson flung glue at the canvas, then sand, and used the randomly–textured
surface as the starting point for his picture.

Most surrealist painters, however, and all the ones associated with Edward James,
quickly abandoned experimental techniques, forgot about automatism and applied
old–fashioned painterly skills to the pursuit of the Freudian ideal in surrealism. They
sat in darkened rooms to try and induce that state between sleep and waking when
dreams float up. They released secret erotic fantasies. They created grotesque
creatures, mapped dream–like landscapes and showed people frozen in incongruous
predicaments.

Edward was always drawn to artists who were not yet well established, who were
still young – in other words, his own age or up to ten years older. He avers that he
couldn't afford to patronize better–known names, but he would be unfair to himself
if he did not admit he enjoyed discovery for its own sake. He owns only one or two
Picasso drawings although Picasso was a contributor to *Minotaure*. Surrealists of the
seniority of Max Ernst hardly figure in his collection, only, from a later period in his
life, Ernst's protégée Leonora Carrington. While greatly admiring the luscious nudes
of Paul Delvaux who wait so unconcernedly in empty railway stations or night
streets, he has only one himself. He does own some fine works by Leonor Fini,
including the disturbing *Figures on a Terrace* of 1938, two men and three tousled girls
apparently recovering from an orgy whose exact nature defies speculation. But the
two painters with whom his name will always be linked are Salvador Dali and René
Magritte.

Magritte (1898–1967), like Delvaux a Belgian, Edward first admired from a
distance, then got to know through Dali. They became friends. 'What a nice man he
was,' says Edward, in what must be almost his only unqualified testimonial to a fellow
human being. Magritte came to stay at Wimpole Street and was charged with a
commission that has now become legendary. Edward had four tall looking glasses
with lunettes by Boucher depicting the four seasons. They had come from his
father's town house in Bryanston Square. After Magritte had finished with them

they were set up on the handsome staircase at Number 35; visitors there remember vividly the moment when Edward would press a switch and what they had thought to be rather dark mirrors were suddenly lit from behind to reveal four new, and complementary, pictures by the Belgian. Magritte added to the surrealist vision a strong metaphysical quality. He took everyday reality and gave it a disconcerting inversion, as in the much-mentioned 'portrait' of Edward gazing into a mirror; you see the back of the subject's head, and reflected in the glass, the back of his head again. A similar picture slots Magritte's own features into a cut-out at the back of the head. In a third, Edward's face has become a blur of light.

Edward was the model for Magritte's celebrated *Le Reproduction Interdit*. He used it as a frontispiece for two of his privately published books. (*Edward James Foundation*)

One of the best-known Magrittes, *Time Transfixed*, is an almost photographic account of a fireplace in a sparsely furnished room. The marble surround, the wall panelling each side of it, the clock that stands on the marble top, its reflection – a proper reflection this time – in the overmantel mirror, the graining of the floorboards, are all meticulously detailed. Through the blank partition sealing off the hearth projects a steam locomotive, its plume of smoke drawn up the chimney. The whole effect is so solid, so matter-of-fact, that when an Irish journal recently came across old photographs of a bizarre rail accident in Dublin, with just such a locomotive poking out over the street, it wondered if the incident might have been Magritte's inspiration, and reproduced his picture alongside the actuality. Someone sent Edward a copy; far from scoffing, he rather enjoyed the supposition.

The appeal that Magritte and Delvaux and the others have for Edward lies partly in this solidity, this professional competence. He loathes abstract painting and though an amateur himself he can't stand amateurishness in others. To be a surrealist painter of the kind he admires you have first to be a superb realist. Beyond this, and beyond the accident that they happened to be up and coming (and, as he says, available) when he was engaged in the art world, the surrealists' imagery and the surrealists' philosophy attracted him strongly. Since infancy he had loved dreams, fantasies, magic worlds. As a rich man disbarred from making a name for himself by the approved dogged struggle, he welcomed the rejection of the ordinary rules and the pursuit of chance. As someone who hated routine or committing himself ahead, he embraced the idea of dedicating his life to the unexpected.

FOURTEEN

According to Dali's biography he met Edward James for the first time in 1935. Edward's recollection suggests a somewhat earlier date. He says he was still married to Tilly and staying with a friend of hers in Spain, the painter José Maria Certes. When Edward kept on enthusing about Dali's work, Certes offered to take him along the coast, by boat, to meet his hero. At all events, Edward extended his usual impulsive hand of friendship, and apparently the two men did get on very well. Edward tells a long and not particularly edifying story about a train journey from Spain to Ravello, with Dali and his beloved Gala. They became regular guests at the Villa Cimbrone. Also aboard the train was Edward's then secretary, a prim English-woman already bemused by this mad Spaniard and his garden dotted with grotesque sculpture.

Gala had gone to the restaurant car. Through the open windows of the compartment Edward and Dali saw a church with a weathercock aloft, turning in the breeze. At this moment the church clock chimed six. By a species of telepathy, says

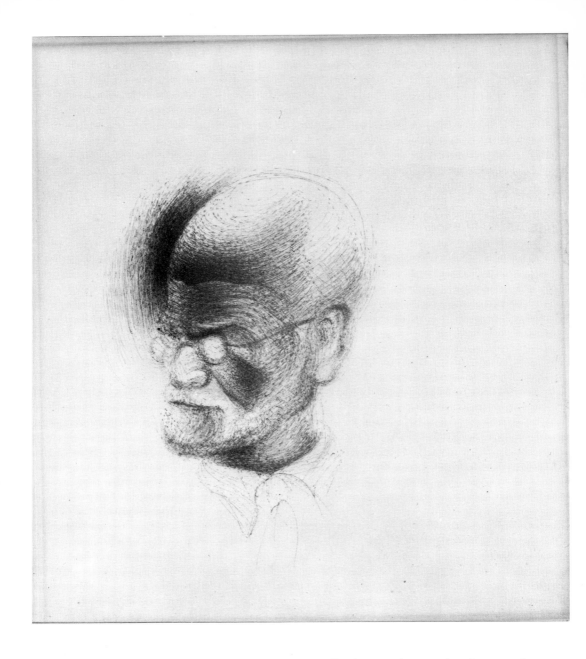

Edward, they simultaneously crowed cockadoodle-doo with straight faces, and repeated the performance on the hour, every hour, for the rest of the journey. Two years later Edward overheard the secretary entertaining friends to tea in her flat at the top of the Wimpole Street house. She was saying, 'This you *won't* believe, but he crows at me in the train, he and his friend.'

Dali was three years older than Edward. After art school he experimented with various styles, conventionally enough; pointilliste in 1923, Cubist in 1924, a Vermeer-like realism in 1925. A marvellous landscape of 1926 introduces an air of mystery for the first time. By 1928 he was a thoroughgoing surrealist, though not officially accepted into the movement until 1934. He will forever be associated in the popular image with droopy watches draped over leafless branches against a deserted seashore

Dali's sketch of Freud. 'To him I was a case, not a person,' the artist and supreme egotist wrote later. 'His snail's skull had not sensed my intuitions or my intimate strength.' Edward didn't rate a mention at all. (*Edward James Foundation*)

background (the actual picture containing all these elements was *The Persistence of Memory*, 1931) or, as Edward's friend Lord Berners put it,

> On the pale yellow sands there's a pair of clasped hands,
> And an eyeball entangled in string,
> And a bicycle seat and a plate of raw meat,
> And a thing that is hardly a thing.

But his astonishing imagination and draughtsmanship extend infinitely. And more than any other surrealist painter (which is what completed his appeal for Edward) he acted out the role of surrealist painter, with his preposterous moustaches, flamboyant appearance, loud pronouncements, staged happenings and public proclamations, such as the 1939 'Declaration of the Independence of the Imagination and the Rights of Man to His Own Madness.' A passionate love life with his model, chatelaine and wife Gala, whom he once said he loved more than his mother or his father or his idol Picasso, even more than he loved money, afforded a final cherry on the icing.

At Wimpole Street in 1936 Dali and Edward planned a surrealist dinner party in such deplorable taste, in every sense of the word, that it is just as well it seems never to have taken place. The table centrepiece was to have consisted of dwarfs holding candelabra which, at a given signal, they were supposed to raise or lower. The dwarfs proved too difficult to drill to Dali's standards and the idea was abandoned, together with the proposed menu of oysters ostensibly chilled in ice but actually smoking hot and sitting on hot rock salt, followed by fish-skins stuffed with sirloin steak, potato jackets containing pease pudding and carrots masquerading as peas.

In 1938 the two of them had a celebrated meeting with the surrealists' spiritual father, Sigmund Freud, who had fled Hitler's Austria and was living in St John's Wood, London. Another refugee, the writer Stefan Zweig, had read *The Gardener Who Saw God* and was particularly impressed, he told Edward, by the account of the vision. Would he like to meet the great interpreter of dreams with a view to writing a book about him? The way to go about it would be to be analysed by Freud oneself. Edward took along Dali and Dali took along his *Metamorphosis of Narcissus*, which Edward owned, a hand bedded in a spectral landscape with ants crawling up the thumb. Freud studied it for some time and then said only *Warum die Ameisen?*, 'Why the ants?' Dali made sketches which yielded a pair of famous ink portraits of the old man. Freud told Zweig that he had never seen such an archetypal Spaniard, what a fanatic! Edward found himself the onlooker and never pursued the analysis or the book.

All the while he had been acquiring Dalis, from great canvases like *The Metamorphosis of Narcissus* and *Autumn Cannibalism* to a little, but much-prized, extemporization when Edward once spluttered ink from his fountain pen on to a sheet of clean blotting paper and Dali said, 'Give me that' and proceeded to turn it into a little landscape with a hill, vineyards, butterflies and sailing ships on the sea. Now, worried because he thought Dali was dissipating his energy into too many pot-boilers to pay

Dali's *The Metamorphosis of Narcissus:* Narcissus appears three times in the
picture – posed on a plinth in the background, fatally kneeling to study his
reflection in the pool, and emerging as the stone hand with the ants that intrigued
Freud. (*Edward James Foundation*)

for his (and Gala's) increasingly extravagant mode of life, he struck an extraordinary
deal with the painter. If Dali would concentrate only on more heartfelt works he
would guarantee to buy a year's output (with a minimum of one large painting, one
small and ten drawings) at a price which would give Dali the income he needed.
Whether this was an act of inspired patronage or simply an investor protecting his
investment is hard to say, because war intervened, and although Edward was already
in America and Dali reached there in 1940, the fruits of the deal had to be left in
France and fell into the hands of the Germans. Edward eventually recovered only two
of the twelve works, one of them having been melodramatically saved – complete
with bullet hole – from the last trainload of loot heading for the Reich.

   He had nevertheless amassed a fantastic collection of surrealist art, however much
he may deplore the description. In the last Magritte retrospective in London more
than a dozen pictures were his. The great Dali exhibition of 1970–71 in Rotterdam
was actually designated 'Exposition Dali, avec la collection de Edward F. W. James'.
No less than twenty-three oils and eleven ink or wash drawings were acknowledged
either to him personally or to the James Foundation. Then are the innumerable
Tchelitchews, the Finis, the Leonora Carringtons, the odd Bérard, Cocteau, Paul
Nash, Delvaux, Picasso, plus some discoveries who didn't turn out quite trumps, like
the German Jorg von Reppert-Bismarck, and a host of curiosities and minor masters
from every age. When they are not on the road with some exhibition the legendary
works are stored in vaults in the south of England. Some are on permanent loan to
the Tate or other galleries. A steady proportion has been sold over the years to finance
West Dean College and miscellaneous James enthusiasms. The lesser items are all over

Leonora Carrington (b. 1917) was another talented young girl who attached herself to the Surrealists, specifically Max Ernst. During the War she moved to America, then Mexico, where Edward and she became great friends. As well as painting (this is *Cock-crow*) she has published short stories and a novel, *The Hearing Trumpet*. (*Edward James Foundation*)

Edward admired Paul Nash (1896–1946) without knowing him as closely and personally as the younger artists he cultivated. He was a landscape painter who was strongly influenced by the Surrealists and exhibited with them. This is *Harbour and Room*. (*Edward James Foundation*)

The famous sofa to the shape of Mae West's lips. Various versions exist but Edward's at Monkton House was indubitably the first. (*Daily Telegraph Colour Library*)

the place, some in Edward's various houses, some hanging in West Dean offices, some in Mexico, some in store in America. Their owner seems genuinely unproprietorial about the whole lot.

FIFTEEN

Edward had made his mind up by the end of 1935 that West Dean was too big and costly to run for a single man, however gregarious. It would be let. He embarked on the conversion of Monkton House as his country home and, egged on by his artist cronies, thereby created the first surrealist abode. Dali designed a famous pair of sofas to the shape of Mae West's lips, Tchelitchew suggested the dark blue and yellow décor of one room when Edward appeared one morning in a dark blue suit with a cowslip in his buttonhole. Syrie Maugham was officially the interior decorator, but the final effect of a mad potentate's private brothel furnished with extravagant jokes, treasures and thirties *kitsch* is Edward's and Edward's alone.

To seal the outrage for those ready to be outraged, the original shooting lodge which he virtually effaced was by Sir Edward Lutyens, the admired architect of small country houses in an enlightened folksy style. Lutyens was to building what Sir Edward Elgar was to music, and Edward disliked Monkton's mousy good taste as much as its little windows and (he claims) its damp and cold and the dim memories it held for him of being bundled thither whenever the big house was given over to a grand party. Mrs Willie had already added an excrescence to the design in the form of a bathroom. Edward had no compunction about adding another for the sake of symmetry. He made the upstairs windows at least seem a little more useful by underhanging them with plaster mouldings in the shape of towels hung out to dry. He replaced what he considered were ugly iron downpipes with mock-bamboo ones bought from a house in Regent's Park that was being demolished. He flanked the front door with two full-size palm trees carved from wood, an idea he borrowed from a rococo pavilion he'd once seen in southern Germany. The fine brickwork in Tudor herring-bone patterns poor Sir Edward loved so much – nine-tenths of it he rendered in cement, and when he decided that white did not harmonize with the surrounding woodlands, sought to paint it the colour of copper beeches instead. All that survives of Lutyens today is a little porch or passageway in herring-bone brick.

From West Dean you follow a private road built by Willie James in order to take his guests shooting by new-fangled motor-car, still innocently called 'the motor road'. It passes through the fields and farms of the estate to a remote corner. There are two gates on the way, one of which opens and closes automatically. The first glimpse of the house is end-on, nestling in the trees, which makes it look very small. In fact it has six bedrooms, four or five downstairs rooms, usual offices. The first

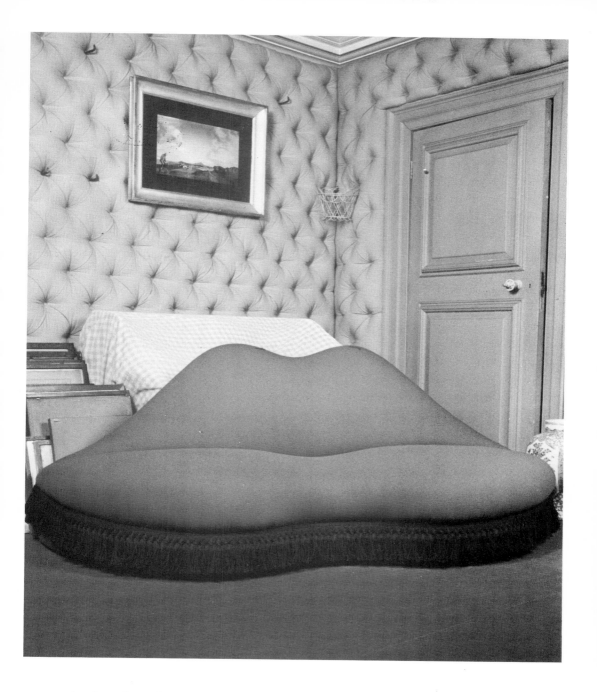

shock is the colour: if the copper beeches ideal was ever achieved, it has by now turned to a blotchy purple. But the carved palm trees, rotted by forty years of damp, have been replaced by durable fibreglass simulacra moulded from the originals, and in the garden is a newly-built peacock roosting-house, with pillars to the same palm-tree conceit, to house some of the rare and, it must be admitted, sometimes seedy birds which represent one of Edward's odder passions. There are statues whose modesty is preserved by natural draperies of ivy, a wartime air-raid shelter converted into a sauna bath, loudspeakers on the roof which used to blast the Third Programme in Edward's direction when he was gardening.

Inside, until such time as Edward feels free to come and live there again – inside, it is Tutankhamun's tomb, the Sleeping Beauty's palace, the ghost train out of season. The rooms are shuttered, sounds are muffled, a musky smell hangs in the air, for against the imagined cold and damp all those years ago Edward or Syrie Maugham or someone decided to quilt all the interior walls with silk and worsted. It proved a promised land for moths, so every six months the experts have to come and let off chemical bombs. Because of the risk of burglary, the windows are seldom opened

Chair with outstretched arms and, on the wall, the
Delvaux *Les Belles de Nuit*. Edward admires Delvaux
enormously but acquired only this one specimen of
his work. (*Daily Telegraph Colour Library*)

and the stuff never quite clears away. You pick your way through the gloom,
through the smell, past shrouded furniture and unpacked crates and stacks of
pictures, moved out of West Dean House ten years since or retrieved from Wimpole
Street more like thirty years ago, and still to be sorted out. Here is a lamp made from
a boa-constrictor shot by Uncle Frank before the elephant got him; here is another
lamp made by the surrealist sculptor Giacometti, glass with ivy twined around; here
are the Mae West sofas, under wraps; here is a Dali on the wall and for heaven's sake
it is *Le Pharmacien d'Ampurdan ne cherchant absolument rien*, oil on board, 30 by 52 cm,
No. 48 in that definitive Rotterdam catalogue.

The stair-carpet is green with a pattern of pawmarks, woven (like the one from
Tilly's wet footprint at West Dean) from the actual prints of an Irish wolfhound
Edward once owned, but for practical rather than romantic reasons – against such a
design unsought, natural, muddy pawmarks wouldn't show up. The bedrooms open
from a strange windowless corridor, hard to spot at first because the doors are hung
with the same stuff as the walls. The Ivy Room has ivy wallpaper and ivy motifs
everywhere. Edward's room has a fourposter whose posts, like the peacock-house
pillars and great front-door guardians, are palm trees; his bathroom has a translucent
alabaster domed ceiling, an alabaster window and an alabaster wall which lights up
with sun and moon effects. In the Green Bathroom, off the Green Bedroom, a sunken
mirror rises sluggishly at the touch of a button and the medicine cabinet is disguised
as a bookcase full of books. In every room the waste-paper and laundry baskets are
in fact of flimsy metal, printed with the facsimiles of *Life* magazine covers whose dates
you hardly need to stoop and read. They're all 1937, the year Edward moved in.

Downstairs again the Map Room is so called because one entire wall is covered
with an enormous map. It is not of the world, nor of Europe. It is not of Italy or
anywhere else where Edward has been happy. It is a map of Spain, where that same
year the Civil War was capturing everyone's attention. Although Edward came back
to Monkton regularly throughout the late forties, fifties and early sixties, and though
he still spends a few weeks there when he can, in recent years he has tended to live and
entertain in the kitchen, a spacious, cheerful room warmed by a pair of Aga cookers.
The rest of the house cannot avoid seeming a mausoleum to the world of Edward
James of forty years ago.

SIXTEEN

About this time Edward's urge for self-expression led him also to a flirtation with
popular journalism, in the person of Lord Beaverbook. Since he knew everyone and
was forever telling amusing stories about them, might he not be of some use to the
Evening Standard and *Daily Express*? The arrangement did not work out entirely

satisfactorily – Edward remembers being summoned to Beaverbrook's suite in the Ritz in Paris and told that his style was far too flowery, too literary. 'Why can't you write the story like you told it to me over the dinner table last night?' growled Beaverbrook, and taking up the trumpet mouthpiece of his famous Dictaphone he recorded instructions to be relayed to Fleet Street: 'The following information will be added to Mr James's article . . .'

But there was one notable triumph. Edward had sub-let the Villa Cimbrone for a few weeks to Greta Garbo, who arrived there, to the excitation of the world's gossip columnists, with Leopold Stokowski. From privileged information gathered from his servants, Edward was able to disclose that far from being romantic lovers, the two slept in opposite wings of the villa, and their intimacy was confined to calisthenics on

Monkton House: the glimpse of rustic brickwork in the centre cloister is pretty well all that survives of the original Lutyens. Note the moulded draperies below the upstairs windows and the bamboo-like drainpipes. (*Sunday Times*)

Sun and moon shine through the onyx walls of Edward's bathroom to illuminate his shaving mirror in the shape of the Earth. Alas, he grew a beard a year after it was completed. (*Sunday Times*)

the lawn, during which Garbo had been heard to reprove the great musician, 'Vun, two, three, four – Mr Stokowski, can you not keep time?' Edward later expanded the story into a *New Yorker* piece which appeared above a pen-name he had lately borrowed from West Dean's former owners, 'Edward Selsey'.

His poetic output had meanwhile continued steadily. *Minotaure*'s issue No. 8, in 1936, carried a trio of surrealist poems, *Les Trois Sécheresses* (The Three Droughts) with illustrations by Dali, which were later set to music by Poulenc. His self-publishing had also continued. After *The Next Volume* came *Reading into the Picture*, a fairy-tale epic stemming from those childhood mornings when he lay in bed constructing fantasies around a picture of a mediaeval city which hung on his nursery wall:

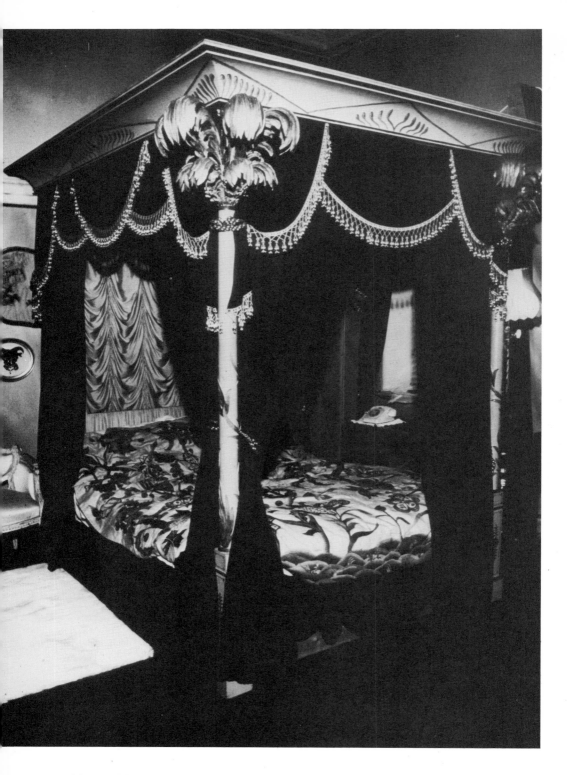

Child, would you enter this fantastic town
whose walls are yellow and whose roofs are brown.
A bridge, full-arched, can lead you to the gate
over a river which is still in spate.

Edward's four-poster, modelled on Napoleon's
hearse, continues the palm-tree motif on the exterior.
(*Sunday Times*)

The title drawing to *Reading into the Picture* defines the dominant dream of
Edward's life from his earliest memories – the dream of a secret walled city to
which he can magically escape. It occurs again in his own pictures of the 'little
city of Seclusia' and in a way it is what he is building in Mexico. (*Robin
Constable*)

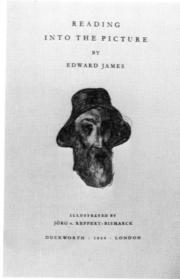

Jorg von Reppert-Bismarck,
who furnished that design
and also this title-page
illustration, was a
descendant of the Iron
Chancellor whom Edward
patronised in the
mid-Thirties. (*Robin
Constable*)

As always with Edward, three good lines and then a flat-footed one. But the
romantic, perfect city is a refuge which has recurred in Edward's dreams. When later
in life he began to paint, under Leonora Carrington's influence, he made several
versions of a painting called *The Little City of Seclusia*. And in Mexico now, it
would be argued, he is attempting to build Seclusia. Though bearing Duckworth's
imprint *Reading into the Picture* was a private, limited edition. So was *So Far So Glad*,
which marked 'Edward Selsey's' début, a painfully jocular prose romance featuring
Princess Frigidaire, allusions to advertising fads of the day and even a reference to Jew-
baiting in Nazi Germany. The James Press was reborn for the same author's *Rich
Man, Poor Man, Beggarman, Wop*, (1937–38), a nondescript collection of letters,
whimsy, verse and a long story about Mussolini's dog which arbitrarily breaks off
and is resumed in a subsequent volume, *Propaganda an International Dog*. Again it is a
good idea – the dog eventually meets Mrs Chamberlain's Pekinese and helps effect a
détente – but the writing is incredibly discursive, ill-organized and sententious. After
forty years the volumes still have the smell and feel of a rich man's self-indulgence,
with their fine binding, gold-decked paper, bizarre typography, coloured punctua-
tion marks, indiscriminate use of illustrations, and prevailing archness. Magritte's
picture of the back of Edward's head is used both times as a frontispiece (with wildly
differing colour reproduction). 'The author's reflexion illudes him in the mirror,' the
caption to the first reads, ' – Portrait of Mr Selsey by R.M.' The pretentious spelling,
the arch anonymity that is not anonymity say it all. What could a struggling author

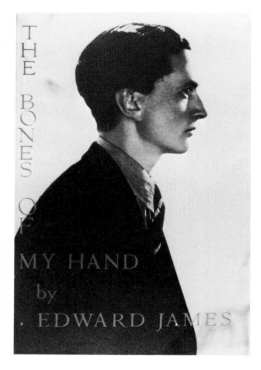

The dust jacket of
The Bones of My Hand.

truly at risk have made of such a production? For that matter, what did the luckless friends and relatives showered with copies make of it?

But then came *The Bones of My Hand*. This was something different again: Edward's final and carefully-considered bid for recognition as a poet. It was published by the Oxford University Press, though subsidized by Edward (unfortunately, as things turned out) in his usual lavish style. For half a guinea the volume included a frontispiece by Tchelitchew, the score of a song of Edward's set to music by Henri Sauguet and on the wrapper an impressive camera portrait, in colour, of the author. The hundred or so pages of verse include some early work reprinted, including *La Belle au Bois Dormant*, a rapturous version of the Sleeping Beauty fairy story. From one of Tilly's illnesses comes *To a Young Woman Under Chloroform*:

> Get well, dear love! Get strong with all the strength
>   that feeds upon the beauty of your self;
> and I will through the gardens of the hills
>   lead you, my white doe, upwards to the brink . . .

From his year at West Dean comes perhaps the most interesting poem in the collection, *Shut Gates*, about an old *seigneur* (perhaps a vision of how Edward saw himself in the far-off future) who has withdrawn from the world behind the locked gates of his estate:

'My mother despised me, And I would blush.
'And that was so terribly long ago.
'My wife is still lovely, they say – but hush!
'She was lovely, lovely, lovely, I know.
'They want my money, they want my blood:
'They've had my love but they've spewed it out.
'They've envied my pictures, my farms, my stud.
'Keep them out: keep them out: keep them out . . .'

The accumulated resentments and disappointments of a lifetime came spilling forth, and most of all the disappointment of the children that never lived, the resentment of love that turned to hatred. The old man waits for death. Edward was not thirty when he wrote it. Alas, the volume that contained it contained also the makings of a last blow. *The Bones of My Hand* was published early in 1938 to respectful, even glowing notices in the *Evening Standard*, *The Times Literary Supplement* and *John O'London's*. But in the *New Statesman* Stephen Spender delivered an attack which in Edward's soured memory stopped him from ever publishing again. 'Mr Edward James,' he tells you the notice went, 'owns great wealth, several houses, a Rolls-Royce, a yacht. He seems to think that he can also buy himself a reputation as a poet.'

What Spender in fact wrote was both milder and more devious. Entrusted with the review of five different volumes of poetry (under the heading *Grocer's Wine*) he proposed dealing with them in order of seriousness: precedence went to an anthology whose contributors included Lawrence Durrell and Rayner Heppenstall '. . . and last place to wit, wealth, beauty, travel, possessions, charm, grace and sensibility, all showered in eightiesh (*sic*) profusion on Mr Edward James, but owing, alas, for their expression, more to the photographer of his portrait on the cover; to Mr Tchelitcheff, draughtsman of his *three* hands, one with bones, one giving, perhaps, the Nazi salute, one giving, indubitably, the clenched fist in the frontispiece; and to the red, black and ornamental type setter of the Oxford University Press, than to the muse of Mr James himself.'

Edward never noticed what might have been some consolation: next-to-last place above him went to Hilaire Belloc.

SEVENTEEN

As Europe stumbled towards war in 1938, then shrank back at Munich, Edward was on a hilarious motor tour of Yugoslavia and Albania with a figure from the past now married to Iris Tree, the giant Count Friedrich Ledebur. They had many escapades involving frontier guards and nights in prison, and Edward grew the little Vandyke

The New York World's Fair of 1939–40 was one of the world's less well-timed parties. Edward backed Dali's *The Dream of Venus* spectacle. Another of his favourite artists, Tchelitchew, designed a striptease routine for Gipsy Rose Lee to perform. (*Mansell Collection*)

beard he was to sport thereafter. 'I suppose you think you're very clever,' shrieked a woman passer-by the first time he strolled with it in the streets of New York, where a beard was then a rarity. This was the following year, 1939, when he accompanied Dali on a last pre-war surrealist adventure. Dali had been commissioned to dress a window for Bonwit Teller, the plush Fifth Avenue store; he was also going to devise an extravagant spectacle at the New York World's Fair, with Edward putting up forty-eight per cent of the capital.

The window display, inspired by Botticelli's Venus, consisted essentially of a

female wax dummy arising from a tin bath of narcissi; though it was perfectly innocuous, the crowds it drew and the expectations of affront the name of Dali induced were enough to alarm the Bonwit Teller management. Gala happened to pass by as they were furtively modifying the tableau. In the fierce row that ensued Edward tried to negotiate a civilized settlement, pointing out that if the company wished to have Dali's name it had also to respect his integrity. Meanwhile the artist chose to resolve matters there and then by storming into the window, lifting the bath tub on high and hurling it through the plate glass. He stepped out into Fifth Avenue after it a second before the rest of the window could collapse on him, spent some hours in jail, but made his point. It was also useful publicity for the other venture.

Edward was much more involved in this, both as a backer and, in the inevitable last-minute exposition panic to get it ready, as unpaid clerk of works and general factotum. The New York World's Fair was one of the worst-timed festivities in

The beautiful Ruth Ford, today Mrs Zachary Scott, in the
Tchelitchew portrait belonging to Edward. The hands spell
'Ford' in sign language. (*Robin Constable*)

history, enjoying a few months' frenetic gaiety in the summer of 1939, then dragging
on for another year while the countries it was supposed to be bringing together in
fun and harmony were either at each other's throats or very soon to be so. As well as
serious national and commercial pavilions it had a lusty fun-fair element. At the
World's Fair Americans saw their first television, and many of them their first
striptease and fan-dancers.

The Dream of Venus – Venus was evidently on Dali's mind that year – was an
underwater surrealist spectacle housed in a palace of fake coral bearing a 25ft-high
reproduction of Botticelli's goddess. Inside was a vast L-shaped tank with plate-
glass windows 30 ft by 20 ft. Inside that was a backdrop depicting an underwater
Pompeii with such Dali-esque props as a door with a zip fastener down the centre, a
typewriter like seaweed and a piano in the shape of a woman's corpse, all fashioned
from the synthetic rubber whose manufacturers were partly sponsoring the show.
The great attraction, however, came from the mermaids who swam in and out of the
setting in long shocking-pink gloves and divided tails executed in the same synthetic
rubber but, at first, with bare breasts. When some of the gamier side-shows started to
overstep the mark, and a 'clean up the World's Fair' campaign ensued, they had to
wear seaweed tops, and attendances fell off. Edward says the real fault was the
timidity of the backers which resulted in Dali's concept being 'Disneyfied'; the public
has better taste than the entrepreneurs will allow and the crowds were always
thickest and most attentive at the parts of the spectacle which remained closest to
Dali's intention. Dali himself had veered off to the Metropolitan Opera House to
stage a ballet. Edward sold his share in the *Dream* and might have returned to Europe,
had not an entirely different circumstance detained him.

The immensely rich Arthur Curtis James was obviously approaching the end of
his life. He had no children of his own. Though Edward was strictly his cousin – they
were both grandsons of Daniel James – the great difference in their ages always made
the relationship seem one of uncle and nephew. 'Aunt' Harriet sent for Edward and
put it to him that it was, however, by no means certain that he would inherit all, or
even any, of the railroad and mining and timber millions. The old man had become
increasingly xenophobic over the years. Perhaps he remembered Mrs Willie's sneers
and giggles behind his wife's back. Perhaps other members of the family had been
murmuring things in his ear. Certainly Tilly had been to see him during the break-up
of her marriage with Edward. Whatever the cause, he had taken against the English
branch of the family and against Edward in particular. As a first step towards a
reconciliation it might be a very good idea if Edward thought about becoming an
American citizen. Edward obediently filed his first citizenship papers.

This, at least, is Edward's story. It is not difficult to think of an alternative
explanation, that with war clouds so obviously gathering in Europe the impulse was
one to save his skin. But naturalization wasn't an essential to remaining in America.
Many Britons spent half their lives there without becoming United States citizens,
and in the event Edward never pursued his application. He still travels on a British
passport. Arthur Curtis James died in due course and left his millions to charities;
not even, says Edward sourly, very useful charities.

Edward was, during this period, very much in love with a beautiful young actress. Since this romance has already been recorded in Parker Tyler's biography of Tchelitchew (*The Divine Comedy of Pavel Tchelitchew*, Weidenfeld & Nicolson, 1969), names might as well be named. She was Ruth Ford, sister of Tchelitchew's boy-friend Charles Henri Ford. The artist, needless to say, painted her portrait. Edward, needless to say, has it in his collection; it shows a ravishing girl with long dark hair falling from a centre parting, huge dark eyes, her left arm across her breast, her right hand clutching the blanket – is it? – in which she is swathed. Her equally beautiful brother expected Edward and her to marry. 'They are like that,' he wrote to Tyler in 1939. Edward sought to foster her career in his usual way. He was friendly at this time with Orson Welles, whose Mercury Theatre company had scored a great success in New York with their modern-dress production of *Julius Caesar*, not to mention the radio version of *War of the Worlds* which drove thousands into a panic. Alas, Ruth chose another, though it was to prove an unhappy and short-lived match. After a spell as a Hollywood starlet, also unsuccessful, she was married again, to Zachary Scott the actor, and in the late forties and fifties achieved a name for herself in the theatre, notably in *Requiem for a Nun*.

Edward had drifted across to California. He felt flat and emptied once more. London and Ravello seemed very far away, Monkton House was fun but it was complete now, there was nothing left to do. His literary career lay in ruins, thanks to Stephen Spender. Why go back? In a sense, he never did. To cross the t's and dot the i's, the Villa Cimbrone survived the war and was used as the location of John Huston's wayward, even surrealist, thriller *Beat the Devil*. Gore Vidal lives near by. Wimpole Street was let to a refugee couturier whose niece was suspected of being a spy. Christopher Sykes adapted the situation for his novel *The Answer to Question 33*. Later the house was converted into flats, then a private clinic. Today it houses the offices and consulting rooms of a medical organization which specializes in bringing private patients to London for heart surgery. Only the lift shaft and one rather unexpectedly luxurious bathroom survive from more eccentric days.

EIGHTEEN

What first led him to California, Edward says, was an interest in mysticism which had been growing in him ever since that vision of creation in the dining room at West Dean. There were reports of a remarkable Vedanta movement, derived from Hindu faiths, which flourished in Los Angeles under the tutelage of the legendary Krishnamurti. Many of its devotees were drawn from the writers and artists of the Hollywood film colony; an active prophet seemed to be an Englishman, Gerald Heard. Edward had been impressed by Heard's book *Pain, Sex and Time*. Another attraction

was that the Aldous Huxleys, who had arrived in Hollywood with Heard in 1938, were bound to be involved, and Edward was also much swayed at this time by *Ends and Means*, a pacifist and philosophical analysis of the world's ills which Aldous had just published. He flung himself into the Vedanta circle with characteristic enthusiasm. He became a disciple of the Swami Prabhavanandra. He attended Gerald Heard's lectures at the Vedanta Temple. He lived a simple life, meditated for the prescribed hours, abstained from alcohol and when lunching with the Huxleys in their favourite

Farmer's Market restaurant (not then the tourist attraction it has become now) would nibble at the same vegetarian nuts and salads, though not without a certain awareness of the absurd posturing. He tells a story of how he took Ruth Ford, now a starlet, there one day for a *tête-à-tête*. The Huxleys were already at table with Rosalind Rajagopal, the wife of one of Krishnamurti's associates. Aldous insisted they join them, though Maria Huxley was obviously less keen. She was, according to Edward, a natural snob who had been weaned away from social and even intellectual snobbery by Aldous's gentle example but had become instead a spiritual snob. A little Warner Brothers starlet was clearly out of her depth in such company. Edward overheard her whisper to Mrs Rajagopal, 'My dear, I fear the poor girl is not yet past the first stage of purgation!'

More hurtful was the attitude of Gerald Heard, an eloquent preacher but a figure whose reputation seems otherwise to decline with every new memoir of the period. 'What can Huxley' – or Krishnamurti or Prabhavanandra – 'have seen in him?' is a constant refrain. Heard applied to Edward's mysticism the prejudice which had blighted every other calling he pursued: how could a *millionaire* be serious about meditation? Discouraged, Edward gradually drifted away, but kept up some of the friendships he had made. There was Christopher Isherwood, for example, and through Isherwood a whole spreading homosexual circle with its own intriguing buzz of gossip and scandal and sulking and scheming. And there was what might be called the Ojai connection. Ojai, a little community up the coast towards Santa Barbara, was a kind of Mecca to the Hollywood Vedantists, a spiritual retreat. It was also where a wandering theatrical troupe led by Michael Tchekhov, grandson of the

The young Jiddu Krishnamurti, hailed as the new Messiah, was taken up by Hollywood so wholeheartedly that he settled in Southern California. Here he visits Cecil B. De Mille (right) on the set of *King of Kings* in 1927. Pontius Pilate (Victor Varconi) on the left. (*Radio Times Hulton Picture Library*)

dramatist, had settled when war prevented their return to Europe, and where in due course a festival theatre arose. One of the players was Edward's old friend Iris Tree, daughter of Beerbohm Tree, sister of Viola and the original – long before Tilly – Nun in *The Miracle*. Another was a beautiful child actress called Daphne Moore whose brother Philip is nowadays Queen Elizabeth II's private secretary, Sir Philip Moore. Ojai's latter-day fame as the home town of the heroine of the television show *Bionic Woman*, incidentally, is due to the circumstance that its producer, Lee Siegel, married the daughter of one of the Vedanta temple maidens, though no one has ever explained satisfactorily why Jaime (the bionic lady) pronounces her name as written while Ojai is pronounced 'O-high'.

At the same time Edward moved in the exalted circles his wealth and family connections commanded for him. His first hostess in Hollywood was Peggy Bok Kiskadden, its uncrowned queen and arch-lionizer, descended from one, if not two, of the founding fathers of the Republic. Through her he met the movie stars: Bette Davis, Ronald Colman, Humphrey Bogart. Equally, there was the growing community of European refugees settling in the film capital for the duration, many of whom he had met in happier times: the Stravinskys, the Darius Milhauds, Thomas Mann, Heinrich Mann, Bruno Frank, Lion Feuchtwangler, Karl Zuckmayer, Somerset Maugham, eventually even Salvador Dali . . .

It must have been an idyllic place then. The smog had not yet started to accumulate in the stagnant pool of air between the mountains and the ocean which today encloses Los Angeles in a more or less permanent blur. The sky was a bright blue, the lines of the terrain sharp against it. The studi lots sprawled over hundreds of acres, places where they started work early in the morning, yes, but finished early and tranquilly as well, with drinks on the lawn. The residential areas of Beverly Hills and Brentwood Park were still separated by tracts of scrub. Sunset Boulevard wound its way through the mansions of the rich to Pacific Palisades and the coast road to the stars' beach houses at Malibu. Red tramcars shuttled along centre tracks now grassed over and trodden daily by keep-fit joggers.

Edward rented houses at first, in Beverly Hills and then at Laguna Beach, a long way down from central Los Angeles but traditionally something of an artists' quarter and also chosen by Gerald Heard for his 'prayer centre'. Edward's sister Sylvia went to live there later, and still does. Edward would have liked to buy his house but already the usual conspiracies were intervening. Friends who should have told him it was for sale neglected to do so; a speculator bought it and asked him double the price; and though it would still have been a bargain it was 'psychologically impossible' for him to pay up. He sacrificed the fitted carpets he had just laid and settled, insofar as he ever settled anywhere, at 6707 Milner Road, Hollywood, towards the crest of the Hollywood Hills. Like many of the houses built on steep hillsides or canyon edges it was deceptive. From the road it looked modest in size, but cut into the slope were as many floors below the entrance level as there were above it.

Edward found a Swedish cook whose breathtaking ignorance charmed him. When the sun set, did it go to China, perhaps? Or Canada? Or did it become the moon? – no, she'd sometimes seen the sun and moon at the same time. He bought a

car, a Mercury, and engaged as chauffeur one of the Ojai actors, Woodrow Chambliss. He began what was to become the ever more frequent, ever more tortuous, ever more speculative process of finding a secretary – no, not just a secretary; the *right* secretary. He resumed the writing of poetry, even if he wasn't going to publish it. He endeavoured to supervise his affairs in England with volleys of cables and letters. He entertained, he cultivated. In short, he constructed round himself again the perpetual motion machine whose only purpose was its own activity.

Edward's house at 6707 Milner Road, Hollywood. (*Gustave Field*)

Aldous and Maria Huxley about the time Edward would first have known them, attending a film premiere in London. In California they had become elders of the Vedanta cult to which Edward earnestly aspired. (*Radio Times Hulton Picture Library*)

NINETEEN

Meanwhile the German armies overran Europe, the U-boat packs ravaged Atlantic shipping, and in December 1941 the Japanese attacked Pearl Harbor. However distant from these happenings in actual miles, Hollywood was very conscious of them. The sound stages of M-G-M and 20th Century Fox and Paramount and Universal echoed to the noise of battle as Dunkirk, Dieppe, Bataan and Corregidor were reconstructed. Familiar figures departed for the real thing, some failing to return. The question has to be asked, what did Edward do in the war, and the answer has to be 'nothing'. Indeed it could be said that his chief concern, as the heavens were falling, was how to get sufficient funds out of beleaguered Britain. The bad news of Arthur Curtis's will had just reached him (actually while on a trip to Texas). His capital in England was frozen under emergency exchange regulations. For a while his only income was the rent Anthony Eden paid for Binderton House, which did continue to reach him.

He was eligible for service in the American armed forces, he says, but classified 4-F at his medical because of his boyhood intestinal operation and subsequent history of ulcers. He also had a crooked toe. He tried for the Allied Monuments Commission which was formed to follow the armies, especially in Italy, with the aim of safeguarding art and architectural treasures, but was turned down. He was in line, later, for a mission to the Chungking government in China that was going to help organize industry; someone else had more pull. What makes his version of events rather easier to accept than might otherwise be the case is that he could, if he had chosen to, have enjoyed a spurious reputation as a secret agent.

Before gasoline rationing began to limit his travels he made many mysterious journeys down towards the Mexican border and who-knew-what destinations beyond. Woodie Chambliss would drive him in the Mercury as far as Tucson or even El Paso. There Edward would board a plane with brief instructions as to which airport and when he was to be met. Woodie would turn up at the appointed hour, wait in vain, and go back day after day at the same time until one day – or night – Edward would step off the DC-3 and climb into the car just as if this had been the precise arrangement. Rumour persists that he was some kind of Ashenden, but to do him justice Edward scoffs at the idea. All he was doing was to indulge a boyish delight in travel and flying, to give a fresh whirl to the perpetual motion machine. Once when Woodie met him off a plane in the early hours of the morning he insisted on being driven fifty miles to Manby Springs near Taos in New Mexico, where D. H. Lawrence's widow Frieda (whom Edward knew, of course) had a ranch. Under the moonlight in a lonely field a puddle of muddy hot water gently seethed. It was, said Edward, a natural spring regarded by local Indians as having supernatural properties, and he had just bought it; stripping off his clothes, he slithered into the water there and then. Reminded of the story, the Edward of today says yes, it is still his if anyone has remembered to keep up the fifteen dollars a year land tax, and makes a note to check this with whichever of his many agents and attorneys might be responsible.

In 1942 his passion switched to the giant redwood forests of northern California. There he completed – or completed for the time being – a sequence of amatory sonnets, *For the Lonely*, and sent them off to the printers (for strictly private publication) along with a preface which put the war firmly in its place: '. . . however universal that disaster may be at the moment, it is after all only a topical incident of history which must pass, thank God, whereas loneliness and grief of love are constants to humanity which even an Utopia could not banish. . . .' However, he did make one private, quirky provison should the worst come to the worst and the Japanese invade. He bought a printing press (after all, an old love) and installed it in the bottom-most basement at Milner Road, ready to turn out resistance literature. When in 1945-46 the fear of a nuclear holocaust became a fashionable obsession, Edward revived and enlarged the idea. Alongside the printing press went copies of all the world's master-pieces of literature – in the event of the unthinkable, the raw materials for an eventual renaissance. That he didn't take the prospect quite as gloomily as, say, Aldous Huxley in his futuristic fable, *Ape and Essence*, is indicated in a story that Edward hatched with Salvador Dali at this time. Their character was a great collector, perhaps of rare postage stamps. How would he spend the last few hours before the deadly fall-out arrived? They decided that he would go on a frenzied raid of his rivals' hoards – he would know exactly who owned what – and as the Last Trump sounded have, for one moment of utter satisfaction, the absolute collection.

With the approach of peace, Edward resumed his travels. There was the 1945 escapade with the Texan sergeant. There were the first trips back to Europe. He stayed at the Ritz in Paris and, because petrol was scarce, hired a little carriage and pony driven by a woman driver. He lived at West Dean for the last time, between its war-time use as offices and its term as a school. So much had changed. London was battered and dingy. Austerity was the watchword. Many old friends had disappeared or been killed, including Basil Ava, a casualty of the last week of the European campaign. He returned to America.

TWENTY

Considering that he now says he hates Hollywood, and was never happy there, it is odd to work out that Edward made it his base for the best part of a quarter of a century. He would vanish for long periods, of course, sending his friends the rambling letters* written in constantly varied coloured inks for which he became renowned. As well as regular visits to Europe, Mexico increasingly attracted him. But sooner or later he would be back in Milner Road, or after Milner Road, Malibu or, more often than not, in the Bel-Air Hotel or one of the Hiltons or even the Holiday Inn, resuming the busy, aimless round as if he had never been away. The hotels were part of the mysterious whirl. Though he always had a home, if not two homes, in the district he would frequently move into a room in a hotel or apartment

*In a letter to Gerald Berners early in 1949 he lists the people to whom he also owes letters: 'Tchelitchew in New York, Sforzino Sforza in Paris, Monroe Wheeler in New Jersey, the sculptor Francesco Coccia and his wife Hilda in Rome, an American sculptor Seymour Fox in Maine, Patrick O'Higgins in New York, Plutarco Gastelum in Mexico, Leonor Fini in Paris, Leonora Carrington in Mexico, Yvonne de Casa Fuerte in Long Island, Florence de Montferrier in Bermuda, Bettina Bergery in Paris, Karl Hofer in Berlin, René Magritte in Brussels and Gaston Bergery in jail . . . .'

house. Sometimes he would continue to sleep at home and have a hotel room for work, or even two rooms in different hotels for different activities, writing poetry at the Hilton, say, and something else at the Holiday Inn. Jack Larson, a playwright who knew Edward well throughout the fifties and sixties, remembers going with him to the Beverly Hilton to clear out a room Edward had occupied months before and had been paying for ever since. 'The walls were covered with letters and cables he'd scotch-taped up, all marked URGENT or REPLY IMPERATIVE. It was the time he was setting up the Edward James Foundation and I guess they were all from lawyers and accountants and poeple, and when they got too much for him, scowling at him from the walls so that he couldn't work any more, he simply locked the door and moved out.'

Then there were brief local forays to Ojai or Santa Barbara, where Betty Harford, from the Ojai theatre, had settled with her then husband, Oliver Andrews the sculptor. 'Edward would come and spend the weekend with us. He was always great fun, loved gaiety, loved pranks. We'd do crazy things.' And every coming and every going, whether for a day or for six months, meant a ritual of packing and unpacking which is as legendary as the polychromatic letters. Every article had to be wrapped in tissue paper, preferably pink, and in the case of sets of things, such as the coloured ballpoint pens, the individual items further wrapped and tied with scotch tape. Once he flew in from Mexico, it's said, with a single suitcase. Inside, a baffled customs officer found only tissue paper wrapped in tissue paper. The converse of this story, told by Paul Millard, a businessman friend, has him arriving for a lunch date only at Nina Foch's, but choosing to arrive by helicopter which landed him on the roof of the Rexall drugstore near by and from which, inexplicably, nine pieces of luggage were unloaded.

The tissue was symptomatic of an obsession with cleanliness (some would say an urge to insulate himself against the world) which manifests itself in other forms. When Edward and his secretary at the time, Joe Le Seur, were working on something of Edward's in the Bel Air, the room-service waiter brought in lunch once and to make room for the tray moved the stack of freshly-typed pages. 'You've ruined it,' Edward is supposed to have screamed, until Le Seur calmed him down by undertaking to type the whole thing out again. The secretaries were a saga in themselves. Should he find some promising young writer and give him this opportunity of earning a living, and perhaps even learning a thing or two, while having plenty of time for his own work? Or should he settle for a professional? In the former category were Le Seur (also a playwright today) and Tom Wright and Speed Lamkin and George Bachman and Friedrich Ledebur's son Christopher. Alternating with them were business-like women, including – improbably – Lauren Bacall's mother. Some-where in between came girls like Anita Starr. The quest for each new candidate was drawn-out and agonized; the selection made, he or she was always the most perfect secretary ever, possessed with unique qualifications and invariably discovered to have some special or coincidental or even surrealist reason for being Edward's helpmate, such as the same blood-group or birth-stone or friend of a friend in Sausalito. After a brief period of harmony would come the dawning realization that the paragon could not type or spell or accept dictation in Spanish, and was not really qualified at all, and then the equally drawn-out and agonized business of disentangling from him.

While the relationship lasted Edward would alternate between extreme generosity and a casual parsimony, omitting to pay the poor secretary until he had to ask for his money, and be reminded of his employee status. It was the same with entertaining. In Europe Edward had preferred to do this in his own home. In America he loved restaurant life and was always taking parties to restaurants. Sometimes he would not only stand the meal but bestow handsome gifts on everyone; at the Imperial Garden, a Japanese restaurant, it might be silk kimonos and robes all round. But once, at a beach restaurant in Santa Monica, when the bill came he pretended to have no money with him and waited until his guests had sheepishly emptied their pockets and purses, and still not found enough between them, before discovering a single bedraggled cheque on his person and solving the problem.

Perhaps it was only a flicker of rebellion against the assumption that he was an inexhaustible source of wealth. Or was it that he enjoyed having power over people, stirring things up? Ivan Moffat, who had known him first in England, saw him now as a gadfly forever trying to sting others into joining in his buzzing round, or (with a change of metaphor) as someone needing to enmesh everyone else in layers and layers of activity which in the end accomplished nothing but helped foster the illusion that he was passing the time industriously. A less than flattering picture begins to emerge, of an impish figure in a well-pressed silk suit, his complexion smooth with an almost brittle smoothness, loving to stir things, rather enjoying mischief for its own sake. He used to enjoy going to homosexual bars late at night, Betty Harford remembers, just to watch the jockeying and desperate pairing off as closing time approached. Certainly he could be either extraordinarily insensitive or extraordinarily dog-in-the-mangerish: when Jack Larson had a play on in town, *The Candied House*, with Betty Harford in the lead, Edward used to telephone her, or her fellow principal, every night before the curtain went up, as if wanting to distract them.

Many, many years earlier, when Woodie Chambliss was his chauffeur and Woodie's wife Erika was about to have their first child, Edward nevertheless made him wait in the car for hours outside the Brown Derby, or wherever it was, until finally Iris Tree stormed downtown and into the restaurant and shamed him into letting Woodie go. When the baby arrived, he was so unobservant that, having seen Erika breast-feeding the child many times, his present to her was a bottle sterilizer. 'We turned it in,' said Woodie, 'for Beethoven's Sixth on records.'

It might be put forward in diffident mitigation that Edward was off the top layer of an ordered society in which (according to a neat encapsulation by Peter Black) you either rang the bell and knew it would be answered, or heard the bell and answered it. He had been brought up in a society in which servants were servants, and though he professed to like American-style democracy he was never adept at its give and take between employer and employee, or for that matter between customer and waiter. When a *maître d'* was once less than welcoming, Edward turned on his heel and never returned to that restaurant; but if after a prolonged absence they remembered him at the Beachcomber's (a Tahitian restaurant) and brought out his personal chop-sticks he was inordinately pleased.

He was also, of course, the product of a society which had considered it perfectly acceptable, indeed desirable, never to do any work. People remember from that period what he retains to this day, the long domed fingernails which in *The Forsyte Saga* are the requisite sign of a gentleman who has never had to do a menial task. What more than anything else turned Edward against Hollywood in the end was that it was increasingly a town which measured you (in the local phrase) by your credits. Everyone he mixed with was either a writer or director or designer or composer or player, or aspirant to one of these trades. Even Aldous Huxley had been on M-G-M's and Fox's payrolls in the early years, clocking in along the writers' corridor for a daily stint on *Pride and Prejudice* or *Jane Eyre*. Christopher Isherwood worked on screenplay after screenplay, besides his books. The actors and actresses joined together in semi-professional stage companies when they had no work in the studios. The sculptors and the potters augmented their income with teaching at U.C.L.A. Edward's name was on no one's payroll.

He scratched away intermittently, furiously, at novels which never got finished, at poems which were perhaps finished but he couldn't be quite sure, he might want to revise, so that although a few were mimeographed and circulated to friends, and one or two expensively printed as one-offs, the bulk of them stayed set in type at a Los Angeles press awaiting an *imprimatur* that never came, until in 1976 the printer despairingly broke up the formes. (Edward, typically, received his ultimatum a week too late.) He concocted a new pseudonym, perhaps conscious of the fact that he was talking away too much of his energy. He called himself Edward Silence. 'Edward James,' he addressed his friends, 'was a talking, talkative old piece of silver, but Edward Silence shall be pure gold. Just wait until he really gets on the gold standard!' Some of those friends, including Jack Larson and James Bridges, are sure that he is a remarkably gifted poet, as, years earlier, was Edith Sitwell, when she wrote to the *New Statesman* in reproof of the Stephen Spender review. Others talk of his 'dreadful poetry'. In a way, both are right.

TWENTY-ONE

It is only fair to record that Edward is also remembered in Los Angeles with great affection. 'He was fascinating, eccentric and possibly the greatest raconteur I have ever known,' says one of his cronies from then. 'He could be a monstrous son of a bitch but equally he could be charming and hilarious.' Stories abound that reflect him in an innocent, Candide-like rôle, such as the occasion he democratically tried out the local launderette he'd heard about. He took along his bundle of Asser and Turnbull shirts and sundry items, read the instructions carefully, loaded the machine, set it going and – bored by watching the drum go round – went away to write a poem or have a drink or stir up a friend on the telephone. By the time he got back somebody had tired of waiting for a free machine while one stood idle and had dumped Edward's finished wash on the floor. Edward re-charged another machine, set it going and wandered off again. When he returned the next time, the same thing had happened. And so it went on, through a long night, until Edward finally found his much-washed washing intact and was able to assume its cleanliness.

Gustave Field, the screenwriter, remembers going to a party at Edward's house and treading on something in the closet while hanging his coat. It turned out to be a Dali canvas. 'Oh, is that where it was?' Edward said. 'I'd been wondering.' Another time he arrived at the house and found the whole place smelling of steamy perfume, like a high-class brothel. In the kitchen Edward was boiling up a saucepan-full of old paper-clips which he had economically hoarded when they arrived on bills and other documents but felt impelled to sterilize before he could re-use. To enhance the process he had tipped in a bottle of eau de Cologne.

Daphne Moore, now Mrs Gustave Field, recalls an occasion when Iris Tree was living in an isolated log-cabin in the brush. She was entertaining friends with a sustained impression of Edward James when Edward James walked in. How he happened to choose that moment to drop by unannounced remains a mystery, but what impressed all present at the time was the touching eagerness on Edward's part to join in the joke without knowing what the joke was. Everyone remembers stories of his decision to investigate a nudist convention (this dates itself, must have been in the forties still) and how the first morning he nerved himself, descended the stairs stark naked and threw open the breakfast-room door only to find everyone else fully clothed; when nudity was general, later in the day, Edward now perversely carried a box of tissues and insisted on spreading one on the chair before he lowered his bottom on to it. Safely home again he reported to his friends that the most inspiring moment was when the assembled nudists stood to sing 'My Country, 'Tis of Thee' and then sat down together to what, said Edward, sounded like spontaneous applause.

His prowess as a story-teller was such that, according to James Bridges, you felt you ought to be paying admission to hear him. He was at his best in a restaurant, holding forth to a party of six or eight. Though many of the stories concerned ancient relatives or London society battle-axes totally unknown to his audience he always brought each to life with a thumbnail sketch, like a novelist introducing a new character. The same stories figure in his repertoire today, except that they are now perhaps even more polished, more worked-over. The handiest idea of Edward's style as a raconteur, with plentiful imitations of fluting grand dame voices, is conveyed by saying he sounds not unlike Peter Ustinov in full flow.

There is the saga of Uncle Charlie (on his mother's side) who gambled away his Scottish estate at Monte Carlo and tried to restore his fortunes as an inventor, only most of the things he invented turned out to have been invented already, and more successfully, such as colour photography or the safety pin. His most promising device was a collar-stud which couldn't be lost, a problem so constant with the middle and upper classes of the day that it inspired half the cartoons in *Punch*. Uncle Charlie's stud had a built-in device so that if it dropped on the floor while being used it would emit a tell-tale *peep-peep*. Unfortunately he forgot to wind up the prototype and on his way to the Patent Office dropped it in the taxi and couldn't find it again. There is Aunt Olive, who although blind and nearly deaf in later life insisted still on being taken on long voyages, until her despairing grandchildren rented the apartment next to their own in New York, installed a rocking bed and a second-hand wind machine from Warner Brothers and transported the old lady wherever her fancy dictated, even – with the aid of a vaulting horse bought from a gymnasium and a few handfuls of sand tossed into the wind – to Timbuctoo. Among those who heard this one in Hollywood was the novelist Gavin Lambert, who adapted it for one of his stories in *Slide Area*.

There is cousin Dorothy (Dorothy Brett the painter) who lives in a shack in New Mexico and weaves her own clothing and, burned by the sun, does look rather Indian. While minding the local store to oblige the storekeeper one day she dozed off and found herself being studied by four earnest travellers. 'Excuse me,' said one of them, 'we were wondering if you were a Navajo, Cherokee or Pueblo squaw.' Cousin Dorothy replied, 'I'm just an impoverished English gentlewoman' and went back to sleep. There is sister Sylvia in Laguna Beach who trained her pet mynah birds to say 'Anyone like to play golf, anyone like to play golf?' so that when her house caught on fire once and the fire-brigade came hammering on the door all they heard was a chorus of alarmed voices inviting them to eighteen holes. There is Mrs Patrick Campbell, whom Edward had known in her last, rather sad days in New York, when her only companion was the little dog she used to take to the park twice a day by cab. Once she cut things too fine and the dog disgraced itself in the cab. The driver, astonished as well as horrified, said, 'Gee, lady, did the little dog do all *that*?' 'No,' said Mrs Pat firmly, 'I did.'

It is not all anecdotage. Edward is also a fund of recherché information gleaned from books and gossip, when his conversation is more reminiscent of that of Philip Hope-Wallace or Sir Sacheverell Sitwell. A chance remark will set off speculation about, say, celebrities who have doctored their names. Henri Sauget the composer was really 'Auguste', for some reason he rearranged the letters, while Darius Milhaud – he once heard suggested – started out in life as Marius Dilhaud, which was less distinguished but really much more likely, he being from Marseilles and Marius a favourite Marseillais name, as in the Marcel Pagnol stories. This leads to a story about the Milhauds in Hollywood and a return to the Ustinov vein to recount, with shrill impersonations, how they wished to impress the Stravinskys, and asked them to a grand dinner. Everything went well until the coffee grounds from the sink blocked the drains, making it impossible to use any of the plumbing. Ordinary measures proved ineffective and in the end a special squad had to be summoned to dig out the drain where it crossed the lawn. And, Mme Stravinsky confided to her friends afterwards, the poor things had *kilomètres* of coffee. By association of ideas he may slide to another French composer, who had better remain nameless, whom he was in the process of commissioning in the thirties and whose wife's diary he happened to see. The entry read, '*M. Edward James est arrivé avec son Rolls-Royce, son Duesenberg et, espérons, son cheque-book.*' How he 'happened' to see the diary is one of those incidentals best brushed aside, along with the sneaking suspicion that Edward James did rather invite such responses with his habit of trying to prop up his verses by buying fashionable composers to set them to music. It was in California, around 1952, that he received his first and last rebuff, when Christopher Isherwood undertook on his behalf to proposition Benjamin Britten. Edward had written a little Easter hymn he wanted setting; he now says that Isherwood's letter to the composer was too cursory. At all events, Britten unconsciously echoed the E. C. Bentley clerihew about Wren ('If anyone calls, say I'm designing St Paul's') to decline the honour. He was, he explained, too busy composing *Gloriana* for Her Majesty's coming Coronation.

TWENTY-TWO

In other arts Edward's patronage was still appreciated. He continued to buy pictures and sculpture, both in California and elsewhere, and he bought for cash, always helpful to the young artist. But perhaps his most significant gesture, in the light of later undertakings, was his championship of the Watts Towers. These strange and beautiful structures in the poorest immigrant quarter of Los Angeles were the work of a tile-setter, originally from Rome, called Simon Rodia. For 33 years he spent his spare time collecting every kind of junk, from old iron and tin-cans and broken bottles to sea-shells and surplus tiles, and – unmoved by the jeers of neighbours – building it into decorative spires and pinnacles, until suddenly he vanished from Watts in 1954, and when tracked down in another town expressed no further interest in his handiwork. Apart from vandalism the towers were threatened by the Los Angeles municipal building department, which declared them unsafe. Edward was prominent in a campaign in the early sixties to preserve a striking example of naïf art, and helped organize a public 'pull test' to prove the structures were sound. Old Rodia had used home-made cement and improvised chicken-wire reinforcing underneath his multi-coloured, multi-textured cladding, but he had welded large chunks of scrap steel into the armature; his towers withstood every test and are still there today, a tourist attraction.

Edward had also helped a couple of painters by installing them in the house at Milner Road. There is a story, indeed, that it was because they wouldn't move out again that he started his habit of living in hotel rooms and eventually parted with Milner Road altogether. He bought a house by the ocean at 31833 Sea Level Drive,

The Watts Towers on East 107th Street in one of the poorest quarters of Los Angeles were saved from municipal destruction by enthusiasts, Edward among them. (*Ikon*)

Simon Rodia, a tilesetter originally from Rome built the Towers between 1921 and 1954 as a tribute to his adopted country, and knowing nothing of the work of the Spanish architect Gaudi. (*Ikon*)

Trancas, towards the westernmost limit of Malibu and therefore of the whole Los
Angeles conurbation. How much time he actually spent there is uncertain. According
to Jack Larson, Edward decided one night the place was haunted and moved out there
and then into a hotel. Edward hotly denies the story while admitting with relish to
other supernatural experiences, such as the West Dean Vision, an encounter with his
father's ghost on another occasion and a particularly gruesome manifestation in
Cuernavaca, Mexico. Whatever the cause, the house stayed shuttered and pad-
locked for maybe as long as eight years. Larson was with Edward when he first
ventured inside again, and says it was like the *Marie Celeste*, with the remains of a
meal on the table, dirty dishes in the sink, drawings on the walls, poems lying around.
The only real damage was a film of rusty moisture covering the floors from a
leaky tap. A day's work by a professional cleaning crew would have rehabilitated it,
but Edward preferred to build a new house for his own use, behind the old one.

He was in any case beginning to spend longer and longer spells away from California. He had fallen in love with Mexico on his first mysterious visits in the early
forties. He went again to stay with a schoolfriend, Geoffrey Gilmore, who was
running his Argentine meat business from Cuernavaca because he was *persona non
grata* with the Peron government, and for a while Edward settled in this charming
little cathedral city himself. Then there was Mexico City, where he had befriended
the surrealist painter Leonora Carrington, who had arrived there, by way of New
York, during the War. Edward also took an apartment in the capital, and even
started painting pictures himself under Leonora's influence. But always he found

Nor could Rodia have known of Surrealists like
Duchamps who liked to impress everyday objects into
art. The Towers are genuinely innocent and
extraordinarily beautiful examples of the impulse to
create. (*Ikon*)

himself drifting back towards the remote, unfashionable mountains which he had so romantically discovered on that 1945 expedition with the Texan sergeant, and where two years later he had bought a thousand hectares of steep jungle land. He would grow coffee and oranges and, above all, orchids. As manager he installed a friend and latter-day travelling companion, Plutarco Gastelum. Gastelum, a strikingly handsome young Mexican of part Indian blood, had been deputy manager of the telegraph service at Cuernavaca and the darling of the foreign community there because of his efficiency, not very common at that time in Mexico; nevertheless passed over for promotion, he was ready to try something new. He bought a house – or Edward bought it for him – in the nearest township of Xilitla, married and started to raise a family; increasingly it became Edward's home as well, and the family his family too.

Throughout the fifties he was probably on balance still a Californian, always returning there sooner or later with fresh stories for his friends of how, to protect his horse from vampire bats, he had hung candles round its neck and the Mexicans thought he worshipped his horse as a god; or of the local witch and her scale of charges; or how, in an immensely long account, he had taken three pet boa constrictors with him to the Majestic Hotel in Mexico City and the mice he kept for their sustenance had escaped, and when an American woman along the corridor complained the hotel was over-run, the maid had tactlessly said, 'Oh no, Senora, they are not the hotel's mice, they are food for the snakes in the next room.'

By 1958 he was deep into bureaucratic muddles over residence permits and customs regulations: a plan to accompany Aldous Huxley and his new wife, Laura, to Brazil on an official invitation was frustrated, according to Edward, by functionaries who stopped him joining the plane at Mexico City. By 1960 he had concocted such elaborate problems of citizenship for himself that he cajoled Jim Bridges and Jack Larson and a third man, Truman Brewster, into a farcical and almost certainly unnecessary attempt to smuggle him back into Mexico via the tourist-trap border town of Tijuana, just across from San Diego. They had just negotiated the American barrier without trouble when Edward suddenly leaped from the car and started running. They caught him, hauled him back into the car and safely passed through the Mexican side. Edward, not to be done out of his dramatics, contrived to miss his plane and keep his friends on edge with enigmatic phone calls and letters until at last he could no longer defer catching the perfectly uneventful Mexicana flight south.

Precisely when the balance tilted and he felt no longer at home in California is hard to determine. The death in 1963 of the one man in Hollywood he unqualifiedly admired, Aldous Huxley, may have played a part. Edward's plans for a craft centre at West Dean were partly inspired by a suggestion in *Ends and Means* that a future civilization might well consist of separate, self-sufficient communities, like monasteries in the Middle Ages. He wanted Huxley to be a trustee but Maria ruled that the great man wasn't to be distracted by such practicalities. Edward thought that she was over-protective; she had been a little Belgian refugee 'adopted' by Lady Ottoline Morrell in 1914. Huxley got to know her at Lady Ottoline's famous Garsington house-parties. Telling stories about – or mostly against – her, Edward always dons a

Edward's original (and surviving) house at 31833 Sea Level Drive, Malibu. Despite the screen doors and clean modern lines the house is quite old by Californian standards. It is also larger than it looks. (*Gustave Field*)

thick Belgian accent when quoting her words. Laura Archera, Huxley's second wife, he liked much better. 'Everyone was very surprised when Aldous married again so soon, and to such a pretty young girl, a 'cellist we had hardly heard of. I called round once and found them sitting side by side and Aldous, then a man of about sixty, reading her Edward Lear's nonsense poems. It was rather sweet.'

At all events, Edward continued to spend at least part of every year in Hollywood or Malibu until about 1966; thereafter with diminishing frequency. On one of his departures he entrusted the second house at Trancas, the one he had built in the grounds of the first, to a virtual stranger, a bar-tender he met literally on the way to the airport. Well, the house got looked after, at least until it caught fire and burned out. The original house remained shuttered until young Christopher Andrews, son of Oliver Andrews and Betty Harford, enterprisingly wrote to Edward in Mexico and asked if he could live there in exchange for cleaning it up and restoring it. At the time of writing he is still in residence but when Edward returned to California at the end of 1977, staying with his attorney Robert Farmer near Pasadena, one of his avowed aims was to sell both places.

You take the Pacific Coast Highway through Malibu, past the 'Colony' where the film stars built their beach houses in the thirties, on past Point Dune to where at last the beach clubs and hamburger stands and gas stations start to peter out. Sea Level Drive is a narrow turn-off tucked in by the entrance to another, private road with a barrier that can only be opened with a key. It bends and becomes a mere lane between the houses and the ocean. This is a fine surfing beach, the great attraction

The 1960 escapade to Tijuana: left to right on the
Carousel are Truman Brewster, Jack Larson, Edward
and James Bridges. Who took the picture is a mystery.

for Chris Andrews and, being off the beaten track, one that escapes the crowds of surf-mad adolescents who occupy other beaches from dawn to dusk. But this particular day the ocean is sullen, breaking in 'dumpers' that topple over on to the unwary swimmer and knock the breath out of his body.

The house is hemmed in by eucalyptus trees, cypresses and laurels, many of which Edward planted. It used to be a ghostly, silvery colour, everyone remembers, but is painted now in the dull red called barn red. A jokey little notice reads *Trespassers will be eaten* with a cartoon of a scowling dog. At road level is only a workshop or garage. The living accommodation is one floor up, though – as usual in hilly Los Angeles – the ground rises so steeply that the far end of the house opens on to the scrubby lawn. Over the slope between, Chris Andrews has built a timber deck or patio. Inside, little remains of Edward's furniture and fittings: a table, the cobbled floor to a little entrance hall and passage, and in the main room a Franklin stove, which is an iron stove of 1900-ish design and probably now an antique. The old square sink in the kitchen and its leaking tap have been replaced by a double drainer. But you can imagine him there in the extraordinary calm and silence – save for the eternal rhythmic roar of the surf – perhaps reading, perhaps working on a poem, resisting the impulse to go and see someone, after all it is 25 miles into the nearest part of town, at least as much in the opposite direction to Ojai, until suddenly the panic of loneliness hits him, and he reaches for the telephone. 'Betty, could I come over . . .?' Was this another reason for finally settling in Mexico? – the instinct that away from all possibility of calling up a friend the solitary man is, curiously, less solitary.

TWENTY-THREE

In the songs of Brecht and Weill Tampico is the kind of steamy gulf port from which the big black freighter will be sailing on the morning tide and meanwhile the sailors are drinking in the waterfront bars or locked in the arms of their doomed, professional loves. It is also, these days, the nearest airport to Edward James's last and most extraordinary world of all. The heat enfolds you as you step out of the plane; by the time you've driven downtown, got lost in bumpy, one-way streets that merge into shanty-town wilderness and finally found your way across the sluggish river that encircles Tampico, you're soaked in sweat. But out on the toll road to the interior with the slipstream blowing in through the hired-car window, spirits revive. This is flat, rich pasture land. Every so often there is an elaborate entrance gate with the name of the ranch, and look! – real Mexican cowboys riding by, with curly-brimmed hats and leather chaps; and young boys on donkeys; and little stalls set up by the isolated bus stops selling beer and soft drinks and fruit.

It is 150 miles to Xilitla but Edward has sent word that he had to go to the state capital of San Luis Potosi and suggests a rendezvous at a place called Taninul, where he has put up for the night on the way home. Taninul turns out to be the set for a Mexican version of *Last Year in Marienbad*, a rambling hotel in the middle of nowhere and now, in what is supposed to be the rainy season, almost deserted. Don Eduardo, as he becomes in Mexico, is sitting at the only table in the restaurant to be occupied, the remains of a meal, half breakfast, half lunch, before him. He is going to be seventy in a few days' time and his hair and his beard, once so dapper, are a tangled grey. The smooth patina of his complexion, as remembered by Ivan Moffat, has now a weatherbeaten look, with the blotchy freckles of age. Nor, as he gets up to lead the way outside, does he seem at all small. He is a rather commanding figure, indeed a bit too much so, he intimates; recuperating from a couple of opera-

Edward wears his Old Etonian blazer as a joke English
milord in the jungle. He likes to be plied with coffee
and tortillas by his workers' wives. Seated centre, is
Plutarco, his manager. (*Avery Danziger*)

tions in Ireland, he put on more weight than he had intended. His voice is strong and
well-drilled, like an actor's or preacher's or television pundit's, with a patrician
English accent flattened by very slight, very fleeting American intonations. 'Romance' he pronounces as Fred Astaire used to sing it; on the other hand 'Mozart'
becomes 'Morzart'. He is wearing slacks and, despite the temperature, a yellow
pullover. His feet are bare except for flip-flops and sooner or later you can't help
noticing the extravagantly crooked big toe which, he says, kept him out of the
armed forces, along with all the operation scars.

The trip to San Luis was a nuisance. One of his peons is suing for 120,000 pesos
(about £3,500) in the courts for alleged wrongful dismissal. In fact he'd laid himself
off and they'd been trying to get him back. Don Eduardo is defending the case,
though without much optimism, the law (as in England) tending to favour the
worker at the best of times, and doubly so when the employer is a gringo. Never
mind, he took the opportunity while in San Luis to see about bringing electricity
into the ranch with a view to setting up a canning plant, and by sheer good fortune
happened also to run into a young cannery manager who was going to come and
advise him on other practicalities. Finally he discharged a long-standing invitation to
address a Ladies Lunch Club in the town. 'Señor James, is it true that you keep
gorillas as pets?' Not any more, dear señoras, and they were only monkeys, anyway.

Outside there are palms and bamboo trees and a big round pool basking in the
sunlight. It looks cool and inviting but a whiff of sulphur in the air gives a hint of the
surprise awaiting the innocent plunger: it's filled by a natural hot spring and is
always at about eighty. Edward says that when his arthritis bothers him he comes to
swim in it all night. He leads the way over to the mouth of a cave in the side of the
hill with a warning to look out for the lethal coral snakes which like this kind of
place, though they won't attack unless provoked. The last case in Edward's area was
about ten years ago, when someone went to climb over a stone wall and actually
put his hand on a coral snake. Twenty minutes is all you have if a coral snake bites you,
as the poison circulates, so the man bravely asked his friends to chop the hand off.
There is also what the locals call *el scorpion* which in fact is not a scorpion at all, it's a
kind of slimy, scaleless brown lizard and just to touch it is enough. Fortunately it is
extremely rare, though Edward says he saw one scuttling away only two weeks ago,
it scared him stiff. In Xilitla just before his time a peon lay down for a midday
siesta; when his mates tried to wake him he was dead; they rolled him over and
imprinted on his shirt was the outline of the scorpion he had accidentally squashed.

A boy wanders along with an air-gun, intent on shooting one of the doves that
are about. Edward wishes him, in idiomatic Spanish, poor aim. Now, where were
we? Oh yes, the scorpion that is not a scorpion. He and Plutarco found one in the
house at Xilitla when it was being built. Plutarco killed it and was about to pick
up the body and throw it out. Edward had to restrain him physically. 'It was still full
of poison, but he wouldn't see that. Plutarco is one of those rational people. He was a
bureaucrat before he came to me, and a bureaucrat must never believe in anything
improbable.' Which leads Edward straight into the story of the haunted house at
Cuernavaca; it is perhaps worth setting down just as he tells it, to give an example of

The foliage grows up through the perenially
unfinished buildings. (*Avery Danziger*)

the fussy yet extraordinarily convincing detail with which he embellishes an anecdote.

'So of course he didn't believe in ghosts either. People who don't believe in ghosts are terribly smug about it. Poor Plutarco really had it coming to him. I had this house in Cuernavaca. It was built in Cortez' time, in fact it was part of the palace of Cortez until they knocked down the wing that joined it to what's left of the palace. All the staircases and everything were very ancient and there were various stories of it being haunted. My friend Geoffrey Gilmore had the house before me and was very amused because his cook and housekeeper had had a man to exorcise the ghost, and the exorcist had come in with a little black bag and wearing a bowler hat and had gone up as if he was going to deliver a baby, and afterwards the ghost was still as active as ever. I never heard anything myself except the furniture creaking a lot, which you could put down to changes in temperature, but the architect John Rex and his wife, Elena, who came to stay while I was in California – I was supposed to join them here – left again before I could arrive, leaving a message, "This house is too full of ghosts."

'Anyway, Plutarco and his mother moved in – it was when he was leaving the telegraph service to come and work for me, and thus the free lodging that went with the job. I was in my room, in my pyjamas, about to brush my teeth. It was just after midnight, and I hear this very heavy tread on the stone staircase coming up from the big living room downstairs. At first I thought it might be the gardener, who was also the night-watchman, coming to tell me that some Americans had turned up from California and couldn't find a hotel room and were going to ask me for a bed, which quite often happened. Or perhaps it was the Rexes, back from Acapulco. But then I realized this was the tread of a very heavy man indeed, in the nature of two hundred pounds, and the gardener/night-watchman was a little old hunchback. It couldn't possibly be his tread. While I was adjusting myself to this surprise the heavy footsteps stopped just outside my door. I was within reach of the doorknob, so with toothbrush in my left hand I opened it with my right hand. Nobody there at all. Lights burning – electric lights – perfectly straight corridor. Nowhere anybody could hide. No niche, no cupboard. Just a rather narrow long corridor, with at the end a staircase going on up to a higher floor and left into Plutarco's bedroom. I put down my toothbrush and picked up a magazine and walked along to Plutarco's room and I said, "You don't believe in ghosts, do you?"

' "No, no. Naturalamente, non." Very pleased with himself, you know. Very smug about it. "No, of course I don't believe in ghosts. I'm not that kind of a fool." So I said, "Well, that's fine. You sleep in my bed and I'll sleep in this room." He'd been sitting up in bed reading *Reader's Digest* – it's called *Selecciones* in Spanish. He took it along with him, but evidently he was sleepy and though I'd left the window wide open with a full moon pouring in and down below in the street – the Calle Galliana it was – one of those modern mercury lamps, he fell fast asleep. And I fell asleep too.

'About half an hour later my light was turned on and there was Plutarco, who was very dark-skinned – he is partly Yaqi Indian – looking pistachio green with terror, and trembling. I said, "What's the matter?" He couldn't speak at first. Finally he sat

One of Edward's foremen, Fausto, at work on an
aviary. ('*Leone*')

down on the foot of my bed and said he'd been woken by five voices all talking
Spanish – gruff men's voices – and a sixth voice begging for mercy, saying "Not that!
Not that! Don't!" – and for good measure Edward adds a few words of Spanish in a
high hysterical voice – 'and then a noise of throttling, and someone saying "Tighten
the cord." It was a man being garrotted at the foot of the bed. Plutarco sat up, and
not a sight of anybody. He managed to get out of bed and, moving *through* the voices
and the cries of the man they were murdering, got to my room. He'll never never
allow me to tell the story. I've tried once or twice in his presence and he always shuts
me up. That comes of not believing in ghosts – you get your come-uppance.' And
he finishes the story as he finishes almost every story, with a little reflective laugh.

TWENTY-FOUR

There is a direct road from Tamuin, near Taninul, towards Xilitla; very narrow,
rather rough, and straight as an arrow across the plateau for sixty miles, but Edward
has some errands in Ciudad Valles, the only town of any size in the area, so his driver
Carmello takes the big yellow Nash back on to the main highway. Plutarco bought
the Nash while Edward was in Ireland and Edward grumbles that it was a bad choice:
despite the size it seems only averagely roomy, and it's far too low-slung for the
really bumpy roads up to the ranch. In Ireland he had a Toyota Landcruiser sent over
for his use from the West Dean estate, which he didn't like either and whose giant
elevation and four-wheel drive were quite unnecessary for hacking round the out-
skirts of Dublin; a pity the two cars couldn't be swapped. When Rover first brought
out the Range-Rover Edward had one shipped over to Tampico so he could fly the
flag for Britain with a vehicle ideal for his needs in every way; unfortunately, his first
trip up to the United States coincided with the introduction of exhaust-emission
standards the Range-Rover hadn't yet been modified to meet. He left it at the border,
flew on to California, then to Europe for a long stay, and by one of those sagas of
miscommunication, misunderstanding and plain mischief of which Edward's life is
composed the beautiful machine remained uncollected until the Customs sold it to an
eager Texan. The only consolation Edward can think of is that it was another
American who bought a Lincoln Continental which he had to sell after a pet armadillo
peed into the air-conditioning system: every time it was turned on the car was filled
with the particularly rank smell, he says, of this species' urine. 'I've often wondered
what the poor man thought when the hot weather came.'

From Valles another excellent highway leads south, ultimately to Mexico City.
The orange groves and maize fields and clumps of walnut trees are lushly green, the
sky is an intense blue, with little cotton-wool clouds. Edward, in the course of a
diatribe against officialdom in general and Mexican officialdom in particular, refers

with sudden vehemence to 'this *beautiful* country'. Hills, then mountains, rear up to the east. Fifty miles down the road there's a side-road off into them which starts to climb straight away in alpine zig-zags. A new bridge crosses a fast-flowing river – the whole road is new, says Edward; before it was built there was only a bumpy un-surfaced track, and a ferry, which helped preserve the attraction this region held for him from the moment he first saw it that time in 1945, its isolation. Another hairpin bend and instantly you recognize Huestmolotepl perking up on the skyline. The name, Edward explains, may mean either the mountain of the hook or the mountain of the needle. Only a steeplejack could scale it? No, Plutarco and his son once did, on a two-day expedition.

Xilitla (pronounced *Hee-litla*) is the contraction of a much longer word, like those long Welsh place-names, meaning 'the place of the many snails where they strike gongs in the trees to make the bees swarm'. At first sight it looks like an Italian or Spanish village huddled on a hilltop. As you draw closer you see that it is more straggling, with every kind of architecture in evidence from adobe huts through nondescript colonial to a weird and wonderful house surmounted by strange cupolas. The centre and also the summit is the little plaza with its fountain and obligatory statue to one or more revolutionary patriots, and the church and the bank and the post office and, on Sunday, a market.

Plutarco's house is at the bottom of a steep, stepped *calle* leading down from the plaza. Predictably, it turns out to be the house with all the cupolas. An iron gate opens into a little courtyard traversed – the only obvious sign of Edward James's influence – by a path of raised cement feet, big toes prominent. Inside it is cool, with tiled floors, tall windows, arched doorways. The upper floors look as if they were added on at different times, which was in fact the case; two storeys, then three, finally these lantern-like gazebos, reached by circular iron staircases. There's a swimming pool to one side, a big play-room and a garage down at the lowest level. At the heart of the house is the kitchen, quite small, a dining room, a little television snug off it.

Plutarco is drinking coffee. In his late fifties he is still a good-looking man, with black hair brushed back from an Aztec profile, but for the last few years he's been suffering from Parkinson's Disease, and though Edward sent him to England for treatment with the new L-Dopa drugs he is no longer as active as he was. Each year, he says ruefully, you realize that the previous year you could do just a little more. His wife Marina is a comely, good-humoured person, as doubtless she needs to be, with five children growing up plus Edward intermittently a member of the household, not to mention anyone he may have invited to stay or those who simply turn up. Once a startled maidservant announced that Jesu Christ had arrived with twenty-five disciples. A self-appointed Messiah and contingent of followers from California had spun a globe, they explained, stuck in a pin and lo and behold! – it marked Xilitla. Edward uncharitably suspected that divine guidance on this occasion owed something to the fact that the Messiah had previously been patronized, until she tired of him, by his sister Sylvia in Laguna Beach. They camped on the flat roof of the garage until Marina issued an ultimatum: 'Either Jesu Christ goes or I do!'

Just now, though, there is only a young couple from Ireland, Patrick Guinness and his girl Liz, and their baby Jasmine, the darling of the teenage daughters of the house and of the little maids who creep silently around like mice. She was born when Edward was in hospital in Ireland in the winter of 1976–77 having two operations for the removal of kidney stones. Her parents would take her to visit him, and he would tuck her in his bed and make much fuss of her, and, showing everyone the great scar on his belly, announce that it had been a Caesarean, of course, but father and daughter were doing well. Now Edward wants to buy them a house near his ranch which has lately become vacant.

The routine of Plutarco's house is curiously casual, at least when Edward is in residence, perhaps from long attunement to his unpredictable comings and goings. Meals appear when enough people seem gathered together to have one, but there is always coffee on the stove and everyone raids the fridge for beer or Orangino. There is no air conditioning, by choice; it's in all the hotels because Americans demand it but Edward shares the Mexicans' private disdain of its noise and artificial, arid chill; the

house is cool without it. Fifteen hundred feet above sea level, Xilitla escapes the
worst heat of the plain. It is now the rainy season. The rain that is supposed to pour
down exactly at three o'clock every afternoon and clear by five is unreliable this
year, but a token shower falls and finishes. The vultures perching in the trees across
the street and, most appropriately, on the roofs of the bank manager's and doctor's
houses farther along, hang out their tatty, bedraggled wings to drip-dry in the
re-emerging sun.

TWENTY-FIVE

One of the surprises Plutarco's house discloses after a day or two is an elegant little-
used drawing room. On its walls hang pictures which in a way sum up Edward's
years in Mexico. Several are by Leonora Carrington, the surrealist painter originally
from Lancashire, but long resident in Mexico City, whom he has known and
admired since the forties. 'Of course, for a long time she couldn't gain recognition.
She was swimming against the tide. She didn't paint this abstract rubbish' – and he
goes into a diatribe against abstract painters, and how anyone can call himself an
artist by slapping paint on canvas, and the gullibility of the Californians who crowd
the galleries on La Cienega Boulevard on Saturday night to gawp at the resultant
handiwork, ending with a whimsical suggestion that all abstract paintings should be
boiled together in the hope that the canvas and paint might melt into a synthetic
material which could be used for making tents with bits of rather pretty colour in
them.

Leonora Carrington in fact continues the Gothic imagery of Max Ernst and Dali
in powerful fantasies such as *La Maison en Face* (The House Opposite) or *Travelling
Incognito*, which are in Edward's collection in England. Here in Xilitla is a lovely,
perilous dream of nuns sitting in a frail, storm-tossed boat with a bird-like prow while
hungry fish lie in wait, though also a very simple white bull on a plain green ground,
inscribed *For Edward, Leonora, 1959*.

Then there are Edward's own pictures, from when he took a studio in Mexico
City and worked away obviously under Leonora's influence, if not her actual
tuition: a fantastic lion by the side of a feathered boy, or angel, in the depths of a
luxuriant forest . . . a bearded, elongated, black-visaged knight astride a horned
mount confronts a creature with tiny Sphinx head, small breasts, long legs and
hopelessly unaerodynamic wings . . . a submarine monster with a tail reminiscent of
the little contra-torque propeller on a helicopter has a hole in its body symbolizing
grief, according to Edward, through which you see a distant seascape. In the background, against a dark sky, a tree spreads crimson branches like veins and arteries in
a medical illustration. They are, um, not very good.

The inevitable Tchelitchew is one of the heads drawn from spiral, mesh-like lines, dated 1950 and, not what might have been expected here, the fine portrait of Plutarco he painted about then. That's in England, along with an enormous forest landscape by a painter called Carlyle Brown populated by Plutarco (again), Edward himself (twice), a party of nude bathers and a trio of soulful women. What there are on these walls or standing on the shelves, mixed up with the modern art and some-how not in the least out of place, are a conventional modern Christ, a conventional carved Madonna with gilt robes, photographs taken by Plutarco of the village or the mountain, photographs of he and Marina and the children and Edward on a trip to Spain Edward organized a year or two ago. They belong because for all its odd appendages this is a family house.

Just up the *calle* towards the square is a half-built house that was going to be

As an architect and structural engineer Edward is strictly self-taught. But if he errs, he says, it is on the side of over-reinforcement. (*'Leone'*)

The Zocalo, or somewhat larger Plaza de la Constitucion in Mexico City. Edward always stayed at the Majestic Hotel on the corner opposite the Palace, occasionally filling his room with birds or snakes. It was there, too, that he ate hallucinogenic mushrooms and suffered an experience in which trees were growing up through his room. (*'Leone'*)

Edward's own, but no work has been done on it lately. There is a plot in Portugal on which he was going to build a house to his own design five or six years ago; as usual, the proposal ran into some kind of legal or planning disaster, and nothing has happened there, either. He has Monkton House but hasn't dared set foot in England, for tax reasons, since 1976. America he has taken against. Ireland he likes, for itself and because he can conduct business in Britain by telephone; he stays with Desmond Guinness at Leixlip Castle just outside Dublin. With his operations, he was there on and off for nine months. He will go again in the autumn. Meanwhile the nearest thing he has to a home is here among the bourgeois comforts of Calle Ocampo 105.

TWENTY-SIX

But his heart, and the last great passion of his life, are three or four miles away up the steep valley he calls his ranch. He is out there every day, as soon as he can get Plutarco or Carmello, who is really a builder, to drive him, often before seven in the morning, sometimes still in his pyjamas, and doesn't return until dark. You take the road back out of the village as far as a wayside *cantina*, or shack selling beer and soft drinks, at the junction with a rough, unsurfaced track. This is the old road which not so very long ago was the only road; even at a snail's pace with the drive held in first, an averagely sprung car lurches and yaws and sooner or later the silencer suffers at least a glancing blow.

A spur off this track leads into the valley. Edward found it originally when

Edward, in Mexican *poncho*, surveys his wooded empire from his unfinished castle, the House on Three Floors That Will In Fact Have Five. (*'Leone'*)•

Whale-rib shapes in concrete, purpose forgotten if they ever had one; behind, one of the waterfalls. (*'Leone'*)

exploring the area with Plutarco after that initial discovery with the Texan sergeant in 1945. He was looking for – well, he wasn't sure what he was looking for: somewhere remote, somewhere beautiful, somewhere he might stay and grow things. Anyone who has had a holiday impulse to find a little house and settle for ever in Spain or Sutherland or the Scillies will know the feeling; if you're Edward James you can act on it. Plutarco had to go back to Cuernavaca and the telegraph office. Edward continued alone. When he woke one morning in his sleeping bag to the chattering, he thought, of a horde of girls but looked up and saw the noise came from hundreds of parrots who had learned to imitate the village girls who came to wash their clothes in the river, he knew that he need look no farther.

The land had to be bought by Plutarco because of Mexican law and he first bought the wrong piece, says Edward. Anyway, it is now in a company name. The spur track debouches into a little paved and walled area which Edward modestly dubbed the Plaza Don Eduardo in the hope that one day it would have a bandstand and a lemonade stall and people would come down from the village on Sunday to enjoy themselves, and so they do, but not to listen to music, while the plaza is used mainly as a car park. To the left is the lowest, flattest part of the property, with banana trees and coffee bushes. To the right the ground rises steeply and dramatically but before the eye can do much more than register the lush green of the trees and the deep pink of the little flowers called *chicos* which spill everywhere it is caught by a curious building which rises from the edge of the plaza and merges into the trees and reappears again, layer upon layer, to fray away in abandoned platforms and fat columns that support nothing. Most of all you notice, down at plaza level, between imposing pillars, bright red double doors ten feet tall but at their widest (for they narrow towards the top) not more than a foot in width apiece. If the man with the key can be found, which he usually can't, this is the formal entrance to the dream that Edward James is realizing here, and the first intimation of the form it takes. 'Why do you make your doors so narrow?' asked the ladies of the Lunch Club of San Luis, for they had been to see what he was up to. 'To keep out fat people,' Señor James replied, realizing a fraction of a second too late that he was addressing a uniformly plump audience.

An archway near by affords an alternative entrance, with only a modest Private Property sign to deter trespassers. A path leads diagonally up the slope with, at the first hairpin, men at work on another half-built house. This one has — but it is pointless to itemize or try to locate in words all the strange constructions on this strangest of ranches; best to recall them at random, as in a dream. All are to Edward's designs on scraps of paper which his master carpenter transforms into wooden forms for the concrete. Walls are as thick as floors, floors as solid as rock. Fat columns rise to capitals decorated with massive yet oddly graceful petals. One or two have been finished in coloured cement, while the rest are still plain porridge colour, and always the reinforcing bars are left sprouting from the end for the next stage, whenever the next stage might come. The only building that looks at all finished is the carpenter's shop, but this is due, some day, to be converted into an aviary. The carpenter will move into the half-completed structure he will share with the coffee cleaning

Market day (Sunday) in the little hilltop plaza of
Xilitla. Leather goods, coffee and striped Indian
blankets are the best buys. Beggars abound. ('*Leone*')

machinery, for the ranch is still in the business of growing coffee and sometimes its
workers will even be diverted to this end. After the canning expert has been –
tomorrow, he said – it may also be feasible to resume picking the oranges; at the
moment it costs more than they will fetch at the market.

Here is another aviary with a big bad-tempered guacamaya, which is a species of
macaw from South America, actually in residence; the plans in Edward's head call
for its considerable enlargement, however, with flying buttresses supporting further
storeys and little birds fluttering between the buttresses to create a kind of bird
cathedral. Oh yes, and at the end there will be a house for armadillos, an armadil-
larium perhaps? The path that leads you on and up is meticulously laid in malachite
and basalt chips, an idea Edward copied from a garden he saw in Granada; a wrought-
iron gate in a stone wall is suddenly evocative of an English garden; the sun streaming
through the wild papayas, castor oil trees, the jacarandas and hibiscus, the humming
birds, the giant butterflies, bring you back to the tropics.

A flamingo occupies a small house with a pool. A second one is for ducks. A gate
you must be careful to close after you takes the path through the little deer park, a
patch of steep hillside enclosed completely by high stone walls; even in paradise,
none of Edward's pets can roam free; if the coyotes and wild cats didn't get them,
local hunters would. The deer trot to a vantage point with fastidious steps and watch
you with enormous eyes. Out through another gate and up to the most ambitious
of all the buildings, the House On Three Floors Which In Fact Will Have Five. This
was to have been, may yet be, Edward's own jungle mansion. It grows out of the side
of the valley, massive platforms already weathered by age, linked by flights of steps
which for all their solidity do seem to defy gravity. The usual fat pillars await
further developments. It requires an effort to imagine the walls and windows into
place, even more to visualize the inside furnished, but at least the view from the house
is already there, and it's stunning. In the cleft of the valley the river drops fifty or
sixty feet in the very model of a romantic waterfall – narrow, precipitate, musical –
before swirling on into the first of a series of deep pools.

Down there, giant metallic blue and green dragonflies skim over the surface.
There are also the giant butterflies, though not so many these days because of DDT,
certainly not enough to clothe a sergeant. One yam-like column painted yellow, one
still plain, rise to some purpose now forgotten, but another slender pillar will one
day be topped by a fanciful duck house which no predator would be able to reach,
Edward hopes, so in a sense the ducks would be free. Of course, there will have to be
ladders up to the house at first, until they learn to fly up . . . on a concrete sluice
guiding the stream onwards he has moulded a head of Beethoven, its nose and eyes
now eroded by the water so that Beethoven looks more like a Pre-Colombian
carving.

Or you can continue up the valley head, via an increasingly difficult climb, to
la Presa – the top – where the property levels off and opens out and Edward is trying
to divert water from the river, by means of a dam of rocks and banana leaves, to
supply an ornamental fountain somewhere below (he could tap a pipeline that
supplies the next village if he liked, but since he provided the link he feels it would

look more gracious not to) and is also busy planting wistaria and cypresses and amaryllis in an experiment to see if more temperate flora will thrive. The interest that brought him here originally was, after all, a horticultural one; it was only when a freak frost and snowfall in the winter of 1963 destroyed 18,000 orchids overnight that he started to build instead. He still keeps a few acres of virgin jungle where no one has set foot for thirty years, and what it may harbour is anyone's guess.

On the way down he says that he overheard a group of peons holding a political meeting. One of them was telling the others that it was all wrong for a rich man to keep deer for his amusement, they should be killed to feed the poor. At present he employs twenty men at 50 pesos a day, which works out at about ten pounds a week apiece. The roll has been as high as forty workers, which made him easily the chief employer in Xilitla. He is also a local benefactor whose good works range from a clinic to a St Francis of Assisi poem painted on a blank wall facing the convent. After thirty years he is an institution, the recipient of biennial visitations by the provincial governor and the bishop. You nevertheless sense what he must sense, that he can never absolutely escape the Mexican suspicion of the foreigner, that among the locals there is still a faint, latent resentment of this eccentric who has made himself their grandee.

As if to reinforce the feeling there is, this night, a noisy wedding party at

Plutarco's house, with music and dancing and squeals from the girls as they try to pin money to the bridegroom's clothes. Neither he nor the bride are particular friends of the family. It is simply that as the owners of the biggest house in the village, Edward says, they have to give these parties every so often if they want to stay out of trouble. It is a political occasion.

TWENTY-SEVEN

Next day is the day the young canning man is supposed to come down from San Luis and Edward is off to the ranch after a quick cup of camomile tea, but no one arrives. Tomorrow, then. Instead, he supervises the mixing of the colour to make the maroon cement with which one of the buttresses of the bird cathedral is to be finished. Edward watches intently as the man steps up on to the bamboo scaffolding and starts to apply it. The effect is somehow different from a patch already there; too dark, too red, too blue, too something, so the man stirs in more powdered colour and more cement and more water. Edward embarks upon a long story of how he had tried to build a duck pond at Monkton House coloured in the same way and how the foreman there refused to believe the process would work and, when finally persuaded to try it, mixed the colour with *all* the concrete so that it ended up only dimly tinted. The peon is patiently waiting with the revised mix. Edward approves and he resumes the application, a square inch or so carefully smeared on with a putty knife, then another . . . how long is it going to take? Anyway he's only mixed one dollop, and will have to match the next lot all over again.

At midday Edward is down at the lowest part, where the green coffee beans cluster on the bushes. Yet another half-built aviary houses some Barbados pheasants. Edward says he calls this particular building his homage to Joan Miro, because the colours and shapes echo Miro's; one of the other aviaries is his homage to Max Ernst. He has flopped down in a chair in front of the little shack occupied by one of his foremen, Fausto, and Fausto's wife plies him with coffee and tortillas, the latest baby tucked under her free arm. On Edward's shoulder is the big guacamaya from the bird-house higher up. He feeds it bits of tortilla and lets it drink from his coffee mug and talks to it in Spanish. The carpenter arrives with a small problem. Edward draws him the detail of a finial on a scrap of paper and the carpenter nods. 'You see,' says Edward, 'he understands at once what I want. In England they'd think me mad.'

The guacamaya accompanies him home this evening. Poor Guaca, he has lost his mate and is lonely, Edward says in the car. According to Konrad Lorenz the species has the biggest brain-to-weight ratio after the dolphin. Macaws don't just repeat things parrot fashion, they really understand what they're saying. Guaca makes small, harsh cries. In the dining room he perches on the back of a chair – one of a handsome

set with high backs – and proceeds to gouge out thick splinters of wood and hide with his bill. Each bit of hide comes away with a loud crack.

Edward's supper is brought in. He asks for a cob of green corn for the bird and, told there isn't any, invents an instant proverb – a town which cannot produce green corn is like a bath which cannot hold water. Someone finds one after all. The Guacamaya tears into it, scattering bits everywhere, looking round with bright, truculent eyes. It is curious that someone celebrated for his fastidious cleanliness, who even now dabs away obsessively with a paper tissue, from a little stack of tissues, at every sign of spilled human food or drink around his place – it is curious that he seems not to mind this dreadful, dirty bird and its even dirtier habits. He says, 'I suppose I have been shat on by more birds than anyone.'

Patrick Guinness and Liz bring in Jasmine, bathed and freshly nappied for the night, and while that lasts Edward's affection is transferred to her. Question: do animals and birds and children appeal to him so much because they, as distinct from grown-up men, don't rip him off?

The telephone rings, which at this time of year is fairly rare: in the morning the lines are short-circuited because the dew clings to the webs the spiders have spun between the cables that link Xilitla to the outside world; in the afternoon the rain does the same; in the evening . . . well, the local exchange closes at eight. This call, just squeezing in, coincidentally concerns the house down by the ranch which Edward wants to buy for his young visitors. The guacamaya resumes destroying its chair. Edward gives it a tot of Rumpopo, a sticky eggflip made with local rum, and takes it to his room for the night.

Seventy years old: an eve-of-birthday snap with the attendant and destructive Guacamaya. (*Philip Purser*)

TWENTY-EIGHT

The weekend brings no cannery expert, still, but some tourists and lots of locals coming to swim in the big pools farthest down from the waterfall. They used to be inaccessible to all but the determined; then Plutarco built steps, a political decision again. Cars, a coach, two crimson juggernaut trucks empty save for the drivers and their friends and girls in the cabs, nose up the track to park in the little plaza with much noise and smoke and the hiss of vacuum brakes. Cans of beer and baskets of food are carried up towards the distant cries of the bathers. Suddenly the whole future of this fairyland seems very fragile. They say that the Çavadonga Hotel fifty miles away is already telling its visitors, mostly Americans, to go and see Señor James's follies. Where the gross red trucks have come from no one knows: something to do with the government, it may be.

Will some kind of Disneyland inexorably arise in the jungle, with souvenir stalls and *Blanca Nieves y Los Siele Eñanos* grouped in plastic effigy by the ticket gate? Or will the jungle, allied with Mexican lassitude, win the place back in the end? Already the colour is flaking off palaces which have only reached the first of three or five or even seven projected floors. The flowering trees grow up through the House On Three Floors Which In Fact Will Have Five. While Edward's enthusiasm switches daily from one focus to another, and fresh ideas come teeming, the coloured cement is spread on an inch or two at a time, perhaps a square yard by the end of the day. When he is away, nothing much happens at all. The picturesque half-built temples seem doomed, at times, to sink directly into picturesque ruins, with no intervening period of actual useful life.

The afternoon rain is heavy. As night falls Edward comes down from *la Presa* by the long way round. The shorter, steeper path has been washed away and he would have been stuck halfway down if he hadn't been providentially rescued by a worker who had gone back to look for something he had lost. The pyjamas he has been wearing all day are streaked with mud. He is soaked through, he says, and will surely catch cold if he doesn't soon have a hot mustard bath. He swears at the red juggernauts roaring and blaring their horns below and shouts irritably for Fausto to come and unlock the door to the Bamboo Cabin. The Bamboo Cabin is the very first thing Edward built here, and where he used to live all alone for days on end, many years ago. It is still there but sentimentally incorporated into the house which rises from the plaza with the thin red doors, at somewhere around the third level, along with a kitchen and a lavatory and almost the only room among all the buildings which has been fitted with a window and plastered within. He hunts for dry things but is distracted, characteristically, by noticing a poem written on bare plaster. It must have been there ten years at least. He shines the torch on it to try and read the words. ' "My house grows like the chamber'd nautilus" – well, that's right. That's a

good image. This house has grown, bit by bit. "My house grows like the chamber'd nautilus; after the storm opens a larger room from my intenser childhood's sleeping place . . . where curled, my head to chest, I felt the grace . . . of the first need to grow. My house has wings and sometimes in the dead of night she sings." That's not bad, that's not bad at all.'

Back at the house in Xilitla he hardly eats any supper, sips a whisky, stares inertly at *Star Trek* (with Spanish dubbing) and *Miss Universe* live from San Domingo on the television, too tired to climb to bed.

But next morning – next morning, Marina Gastelum is with many sighs and *tsks-tsks* unpeeling wodges of household receipts that are stuck messily together and spreading them out on the cloth to dry. It seems that far from flaking out Edward was seized with a new lease of life around midnight and led his young visitors on a raid of the kitchen. In the course of concocting an elaborate hot drink he cracked the blender and it all ran into the kitchen drawer.

Up at the ranch he is as sprightly as ever. In the House On Three Floors Which Will In Fact Have Five – or Four, or Six – he points out the palanquin by which he was transported round the estate when twenty years ago a tree fell on him and broke his back. Today, surely, the cannery man will come. Next week he is seventy. Through the flamboyanes and jacarandas and hibiscus his fantastic shapes and columns shimmer in the sun. It *is* enchanted, it is beautiful, a hanging garden of Xanadu. He has made something which, whatever happens to it, must still be touching some traveller's imagination (in this antique land) a thousand years from now. He has made his mark at last, this often unlikeable, more often endearing, indomitable elfland king.

Edward: an indoor portrait. (*'Leone'*)

I have seen such beauty as one man has seldom seen;
therefore will I be grateful to die in this little room,
surrounded by the forests, the great green gloom
of the trees my only gloom – and the sound, the sound of green.

Here amid the warmth of the rain, what might have been
is resolved into the tenderness of a tall doom
who says: 'You did your best, rest – and after you the bloom
of what you loved and planted still will whisper what you mean.'

And the ghosts of the birds I loved, will attend me each a friend;
like them shall I have flown beyond the realm of words.
You, through the trees, shall hear them, long after the end
calling me beyond the river. For the cries of birds
continue, as – defended by the cortege of their wings –
my soul among strange silences yet sings.

EDWARD JAMES